Customer Satisfaction Measurement
for ISO 9000:2000

Customer Satisfaction Measurement for ISO 9000:2000

Nigel Hill
Bill Self
Greg Roche

OXFORD AMSTERDAM BOSTON LONDON NEW YORK PARIS
SAN DIEGO SAN FRANCISCO SINGAPORE SYDNEY TOKYO

Butterworth-Heinemann
An imprint of Elsevier Science
Linacre House, Jordan Hill, Oxford OX2 8DP
200 Wheeler Road, Burlington, MA 01803

First published 2002
Reprinted 2003

British Library Cataloguing in Publication Data
A catalogue record for this book is available from the British Library

Library of Congress Cataloguing in Publication Data
A catalogue record for this book is available from the Library of Congress

ISBN 0 7506 5513 5

For information on all Butterworth-Heinemann
publications please visit our website at www.bh.com

Printed and bound in Great Britain by Biddles Ltd
www.biddles.co.uk

Contents

Foreword

At last! The world's most popular quality standard now includes requirements relating to enhancing customer satisfaction. Launched in December 2000, ISO 9001:2000 requires an organisation to have an effective system for monitoring its customers' views. Well-chosen statistics on customer satisfaction collated over time are an excellent predictor of future business performance. Happy satisfied customers will improve the bottom line of an organisation. Disaffected ones will prophesy a company's quick descent into the loss-making pit.

Businesses are desperate to appear tuned into their customers' needs. This can be seen in the ubiquitous annual report where it is difficult to find one that does not state: 'Our company is committed to the highest levels of customer satisfaction.' But you only have to turn this bland promise on its head to see that it is meaningless. How many companies are dedicated to the lowest levels of customer satisfaction?

Customer satisfaction is the most common form of market research in business-to-business markets and is often connected to quality and production measurement, rather than as straight marketing-based research. It is essential that an organisation has the will to actually make improvement changes before embarking on a customer satisfaction measurement exercise; otherwise it will simply annoy its customers by taking their time to collect information, then not doing anything with it.

Customer satisfaction has roots in two ideas about quality. First, quality can be measured by the gap between customers' expectations and their perceptions. This gap-based view of quality says that if you beat customers' expectations you have good quality. The second view is that quality is about conformance to a standard or specification. Once the design is set, quality is about ensuring that the end deliverable to the customer meets this design. Thus, customer satisfaction is about monitoring the quality of delivery of the product and service. This was the view of the old ISO 9000 standard and it had its limitations. It overlooked the fact that the product might be perfectly produced but it might not be satisfying customer needs and furthermore that competitors do not stand still.

Although design is an essential part of a customer's overall view of satisfaction, it is not possible to separate out design from delivery. Organisations must be careful to define what they are looking for from a customer satisfaction study. For example, a survey of 100 people reveals that they are very happy with the local bus service but closer analysis shows the majority of these people rarely, if ever, take the bus. The survey result is unhelpful. The right approach to studies must also be taken. One large high street retailer used to measure its customer satisfaction on returns. When it came to underwear it assumed that its customers were very happy, as there was only a 0.2 per cent return. That was until it found that it had lost market share. On further inspection it found that if customers found one item out of five unsuitable they would not bother to return it. Returns are not always a good customer satisfaction indicator.

Most customer satisfaction measurement is conducted using a fairly basic four or five point scale from 'very satisfied', 'satisfied', (neither), 'dissatisfied', 'very dissatisfied'. Typically satisfaction is reported as the percentage of customers rating an organisation as either 'satisfied' or 'very satisfied'. Unfortunately, this tends to be quite a crude measurement. Most companies will score around 75–85 per cent. Even poorly performing organisations can still easily reach 60 per cent. The difficulty is that within such studies the year-on-year improvements are very hard to spot. The accuracy of the study often means that changes of one or two per cent points are within the statistical tolerance of the design and show no real change, yet most companies would struggle to see changes beyond one to two per cent.

Customer satisfaction is not just about surveys. It is worthwhile devoting time to data from alternative types of feedback. For example from sales and marketing personnel, the customer complaints/compliments process, returns/ rejects/etc, service or maintenance performance and warranty claims. This data does not have to be extensive but it can help to build up the whole picture of customer related feedback when used correctly.

The Institute of Quality Assurance (IQA) has long advocated putting customer satisfaction at the top of the agenda. Customer satisfaction measurement should be a driver of business improvement rather than a sweet add-on. ISO 9000 has over 400 000 certificates worldwide. It is expected that the majority of these will move forward to the updated ISO 9001:2000. For many organisations moving their quality management systems forward to include customer satisfaction measurement will be a mammoth task.

Nigel Hill is a regular contributor to *Quality World* magazine, published by the IQA. He, Bill Self and Greg Roche outline, in a user friendly manner, how an organisation can get to grips with customer satisfaction measurement to meet the requirements of ISO 9001:2000. Whether you are considering an upgrade to the new standard or taking the plunge into quality management for the first time, this is an essential read.

Helen Oldfield
Publisher
Institute of Quality Assurance

1

Why measure customer satisfaction?

Summary

ISO 9001:2000 has placed customers at the heart of a quality management system whose objective is continual improvement in customer satisfaction. But why is that? Why is customer satisfaction so important? This chapter will explain:

(a) Why loyal customers are more profitable.
(b) How customer satisfaction drives loyalty.
(c) Why measuring customer satisfaction is essential, though not an end in itself.
(d) The key milestones of a customer satisfaction measurement process that will provide a reliable measure of customer satisfaction and meet the requirements of ISO 9001:2000.

1.1 What the Standard says

ISO 9001:2000 is very clear that the central purpose of a quality management system is to ensure that the organisation provides goods and/or services that satisfy customers. To quote from the introduction to the Standard:

> *This International Standard promotes the adoption of a process approach when developing, implementing and improving the effectiveness of a quality management system, to enhance customer satisfaction by meeting customer requirements.*

The Standard contains considerably more detail on customer satisfaction and this will be reviewed in full in Chapter 2, with subsequent chapters focusing on specific requirements of ISO 9001:2000 that relate to customer satisfaction measurement.

1.2 Keeping customers is profitable

Ever since the American Consumer Association announced in the late 1980s that it was five times more expensive to win a new customer than to keep an existing one, organisations have become very interested in the economics of customer retention. Many case studies have confirmed this view. MBNA rose from the 38th largest bankcard supplier in the USA in 1982 to the 2nd largest by the late 1990s due to superior customer retention and more selective customer acquisition. MBNA selects its new customers very carefully and keeps them for much longer than other credit card companies. It measures customer satisfaction continually and pays staff a proportion of profit as a bonus for each day of the year that its customer satisfaction measure is above target.

Some companies make the value of customer retention more tangible by calculating and promoting to employees a customer lifetime value figure based on how much typical customers spend and how long they stay with the business. The most famous early example of customer lifetime value was provided by Domino Pizza where Phil Bressler came up with a figure of $4000 as the lifetime value of a typical customer. He encouraged his employees to think of customers as worth $4000 when delivering an $8 pizza.

Carl Sewell considered that the lifetime value of a typical customer of his Cadillac dealership was $332 000 and encouraged employees to suggest ways of enhancing service levels to recognise such high value customers. Initiatives implemented included painting the workshop floor white and mopping it every time a car was driven over it to keep it spotless. Customers, who were also invited into the workshop to meet the mechanic who had worked on their car would hopefully think that if they took so much care over the floor, they must be providing a very high quality service.

Keeping customers paid very handsomely for MBNA, Domino Pizza and Sewell Cadillac. It also pays for other organisations. In his book, *The Loyalty Effect*, Frederick Reichheld demonstrates the value of customer retention across several very diverse industries whose customer loyalty economics he studied in depth. Figure 1.1 shows the impact of a 5 percentage point increase in customer retention rate on customer net present value across a range of business sectors.

Reichheld went on to demonstrate why customers become more profitable as organisations keep them longer. Figure 1.2 shows that a significant profit increase is generated because customers buy more as they get to know and trust your organisation. As you get to know each other, the cost of servicing customers decreases. New customers need more help, make more enquiries, complain more and return goods more. Over time they are more likely to buy mainstream products or services that you recommend and, because they have developed accurate expectations about what will be provided, are more likely to be satisfied with the outcome. If they are satisfied, or even better, delighted, they will recommend your organisation to others. New referral customers are

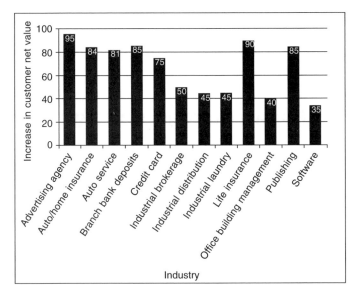

Figure 1.1 The value of customer retention. (Source, *The Loyalty Effect* by Frederick Reichheld, Harvard University Press.)

highly profitable because you didn't have to invest marketing budget to get them and, because your existing good customers tend to recommend people like themselves, they usually end up being good customers who are well suited to your organisation. Finally, loyal customers will usually pay a small

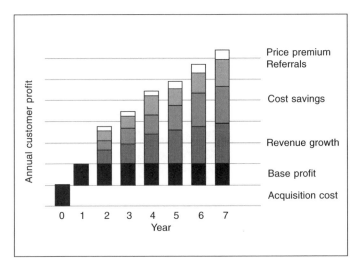

Figure 1.2 Why loyal customers are more profitable. (Source, *The Loyalty Effect.*)

price premium (estimated at 9% on average) because they have become convinced of the value provided by your organisation. Harvard Business School has coined the phrase 'the three Rs' (retention, related sales and referrals) to summarize the value of keeping customers.

1.3 Satisfied customers are more likely to stay

There is growing evidence of the link that we all intuitively know to exist between customer satisfaction and loyalty. Not surprisingly, many companies have discovered that there is a strong correlation between satisfaction and loyalty only at the highest levels of customer satisfaction. Figure 1.3, based on data from companies such as AT&T, Rank Xerox and The Royal Bank of Scotland, shows that on average, 95% of customers scoring 'excellent' or 'very satisfied' (ticking the top box) subsequently remain loyal compared with only 65% who score 'good' or 'satisfied'. Not surprisingly the loyalty rate then plummets even more dramatically to 15% for 'average' or the middle box, only 2% for 'poor' or 'quite dissatisfied' and no future loyalty for those scoring the bottom box. This explains why many organisations that are experienced in customer satisfaction measurement say that only 'top box' scores can be regarded as an acceptable level of performance.

Some companies have put numbers against the value of customer satisfaction. IBM calculated that each 1% rise in its customer satisfaction index was worth $500 million in additional sales over the following five years. Toyota

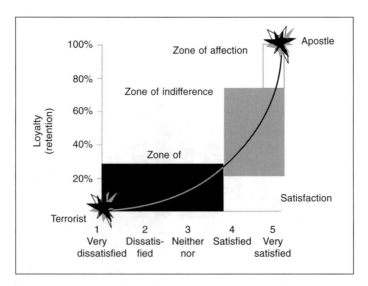

Figure 1.3 Satisfaction–loyalty links. (Source, *The Service–Profit Chain* by James L. Heskett, W. Earl Sasser Jr and Leonard A. Schlesinger, Free Press.)

demonstrated a clear difference in financial performance between its dealers who were most and least successful in satisfying customers. Figure 1.4 shows the far superior financial performance of the dealerships with the most satisfied customers.

	Top dealers on customer satisfaction	Bottom dealers on customer satisfaction	Difference	
Net profit	$102,158	$69,693	$32,465	47% better
Net profit as % of total sale	1.61%	0.89%	0.72%	81% better
Net profit per employee	$1761	$1056	$705	67% better
New vehicle selling expense: % total new vehicle sales	4.72%	5.09%	0.37%	7.3% better
Net profit as % gross profit	12.12%	6.97%	-5.15%	74% better
Salesperson turnover	23.60%	41.20%	17.60%	43% better
Advertising	$79,032	$112,858	$33,826	30% lower

Figure 1.4 The benefits of customer satisfaction at Toyota

1.4 You can't manage what you don't measure

Customer loyalty and corporate profitability are maximised in the long run by satisfying customers. Customer satisfaction is based on meeting or exceeding customers' requirements. To achieve this you have to organise the business to *'do best what matters most to customers'*. A customer satisfaction measurement programme will provide the information you need to maximize the beneficial financial effects of having satisfied and loyal customers. Customer satisfaction measurement will enable you to:

- accurately identify customers' requirements and their relative importance;
- understand how customers perceive your organisation and whether your performance meets their requirements;
- identify PFIs (priorities for improvement) – areas where improvements in performance will produce the greatest gain in customer satisfaction;
- pinpoint 'understanding gaps' where your own staff have a misunderstanding of customers' priorities or their ability to meet customers' needs;
- set goals for service improvement and monitor progress against a customer satisfaction index;
- increase profits through improved customer loyalty and retention.

1.5 From measurement to action

Some people have claimed that CSM (customer satisfaction measurement) programmes have 'failed to deliver the goods' in their organisation. When such claims are investigated, they are usually based on a total misunderstanding of what CSM should be expected to deliver. A CSM survey can deliver very accurate data on customers' level of satisfaction and can highlight the areas where customers are least happy but it can't solve the problems, improve the service and increase customer satisfaction. That relies on decisions, action and a lot of hard work. In our work we have seen a huge gulf between the most and least customer focused organisations both in terms of their speed of reaction to CSM results and the effectiveness of actions taken. If a CSM programme does fail it is very rarely the information that's the problem but the organisation's inability to turn it into effective action afterwards.

1.6 An overview of the CSM process

As well as addressing the customer satisfaction measurement requirements of ISO 9001:2000, this book will explain how to produce reliable measures of customer satisfaction and what needs to be done if those measures are to be successfully used as the basis for effective action.

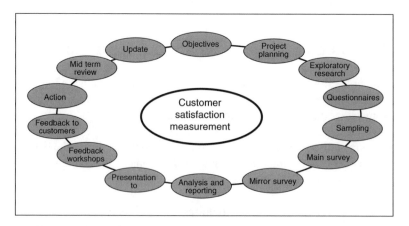

Figure 1.5 An overview of the CSM process

The first stage of the customer research process is to clarify with customers exactly what their requirements are so that an appropriate questionnaire, which asks the right questions, can be designed. This is done through exploratory research using focus groups (typically in consumer markets) or one-to-one depth interviews (the norm in business markets). It is customers' most important requirements, as stated by the customers themselves, which must form the basis for a CSM questionnaire and not assumptions you make in-house about what you think might be important to customers. The exploratory research process is covered in Chapter 3.

Two main factors determine the accuracy of a CSM study. The first is asking the right questions (hence the exploratory research), the second is asking them to the right people – a sample of customers which accurately reflects your customer base. Three things decide the accuracy of a sample. It must be representative, it must be randomly selected and it must be large enough. In Chapter 4 we examine the various sampling options.

Once you are confident that you will be asking the right questions to the right people, you can design the final questionnaire and begin the main survey. The first decision here is to determine how the survey will be carried out. It could be done using telephone interviews, personal interviews or self-completion questionnaires, and the latter can come in a number of forms including, postal, point of sale and electronic. Chapter 5 outlines the survey options together with their advantages and disadvantages.

Having determined the type of survey you will carry out, an appropriate questionnaire can be designed. Chapter 6 will examine how to design a professional and reliable questionnaire including how to select an appropriate rating scale to accurately measure the level of customer satisfaction.

Having carried out the survey you will need to analyse the results. Chapter 7 examines several analytical techniques and highlights some common mistakes to avoid. We also explain how to calculate an accurate customer satisfaction index.

After analysing the data and producing a report, feedback should be swiftly provided to employees and customers. Inadequate feedback is a common reason why some organisations fail to reap the full rewards from their CSM process. Only if employees fully understand the survey results and their implications will effective action be taken. Chapter 8 focuses on customer communications and Chapter 9 on involving employees. A worthwhile addition to a CSM study is a mirror survey where the same set of questions is administered to your own employees to discover whether they understand what's important to customers and how closely they are meeting customers' requirements. Typically conducted using self-completion questionnaires, a mirror survey will often trace the origin of customer satisfaction problems to employees' inaccurate understanding of the customer perspective – the so-called 'understanding gaps'. Chapter 9 also explains how to conduct and analyse a mirror survey. The final chapter will introduce some additional concepts such as competitor analysis that are not necessary to conform to the requirements of ISO 9001:2000 but are covered by ISO 9004:2000.

1.7 Conclusions

(a) According to ISO 9001:2000 customer satisfaction should be measured to monitor the effectiveness of the quality management system and to highlight areas where improvements should be made.

(b)   There is a growing body of evidence that keeping existing customers is more profitable than winning new ones and that the longer you can keep customers the more profitable they become.

(c)   The best way to keep customers is to meet, or, even better, to exceed their requirements. Studies show that the relationship between customer satisfaction and loyalty is exponential which means that very satisfied customers are much more likely to remain loyal than merely satisfied ones.

(d)   Only through measuring customer satisfaction will you develop sufficient understanding of customers' requirements to organise the business to meet those needs and adequate knowledge of your success in satisfying customers to make the improvements necessary to improve customer satisfaction.

(e)   Although customer satisfaction measurement will help you to manage customers, it is not an end in itself. Where organisations have been disappointed with the effectiveness of their CSM programme, the fault is often not with the measures themselves but with how the organisation subsequently uses the measures to achieve continual improvement.

(f)   This book will take you step by step through a customer satisfaction measurement process that will produce a reliable measure of customer satisfaction and meet the requirements of ISO 9001:2000.

2

Customer satisfaction measurement and ISO 9001:2000

Summary

This chapter will review the development of quality management systems and explain how customer satisfaction measurement fits into ISO 9001:2000. Specifically we will cover:

(a) The historical origins of ISO 9000.
(b) The components of the ISO 9001:2000 family of standards.
(c) The customer-focused philosophy of ISO 9001:2000.
(d) The specific requirements for customer satisfaction measurement within ISO 9001:2000.
(e) The transition from ISO 9000:1994 to ISO 9001:2000.

2.1 Background to the new Standard

As products and manufacturing processes became more complex in the years after the Second World War, there was a growing realisation of the need for systems to control quality, especially for military and other potentially dangerous products. The industrialised economies therefore began to develop their own organisations to achieve this objective by producing 'standards' to which various types of goods should be manufactured. The main national bodies, each known by their acronyms were:

- AFNOR: Association Français de Normalisation (France)
- ANSI: American National Standards Institute (USA)
- BSI: British Standards Institute (UK)
- CSA: Canadian Standards Association (Canada)
- DIN: Deutsch Institut fur Normung e.v. (Germany).

As consumerism grew in the 1960s and 1970s, customers became increasingly quality conscious and grew less tolerant of poor quality products. Manufacturers therefore found it helpful to be able to provide evidence that they were capable of producing good quality products and this was done by having formal third party certification of their quality management systems and procedures. The British Standards Institute with its BS 5750 standard first provided this on a large scale. The USA followed with ANSI 90.

There were others too and gradually every country with any degree of industrialisation began producing its own standards. At best this was confusing and inefficient for international trade. At worst, standards could be used as unofficial but very effective barriers to trade. Led by the European Community, national governments increasingly began to understand the beneficial effects of harmonising international standards.

The International Standards Organization (ISO) was formed by the United Nations as long ago as 1947. Its first international quality standard, ISO 9000:1987, was largely based on BS 5750. This was updated to become ISO 9000:1994, but its structure remained fundamentally unchanged from the original version.

In the 1990s, ISO 9000 was increasingly criticised on the grounds that it did not really assure the delivery of a quality product or service since organisations could comply simply by demonstrating that they had consistently followed the procedures laid down in their quality manual. Their procedures may not have been adequate to ensure sufficiently high quality, and ISO 9000:1994 contained no requirement for organisations to judge their quality according to its acceptability to the customer nor any requirement for them to improve their quality.

A three-year review process resulted in the publication of ISO 9001:2000 in December 2000. The three 1994 standards, ISO 9001, 9002 and 9003 have been reduced to one standard, ISO 9001:2000 for certification purposes. The addition of a 'permissible exclusions' clause allows organisations to waive irrelevant requirements provided they can demonstrate their non-applicability. An obvious example would be clauses relating to design for organisations previously registered to ISO 9002:1994. In addition, the 20 elements of ISO 9000:1994 were reduced to four main sections covering:

- management responsibility;
- resource management;
- product realisation;
- measurement, analysis and improvement.

The most fundamental changes, however, are deep-rooted changes to the philosophical basis of the quality management standard, putting the focus on ensuring that the quality system delivers a quality outcome for the customer and placing emphasis on continual improvement. This new focus will be explored in Section 2.3 of this chapter.

2.2 Components of the ISO 9001:2000 family of standards

The new family of quality management standards comprises three individual standards:

- ISO 9000:2000
- ISO 9001:2000
- ISO 9004:2000

All three standards can be purchased from assessment bodies individually or as a set. Although ISO 9001 is the only one that is necessary for certification, the three standards are complementary and each adds a dimension to the development of an effective quality management system.

2.2.1 ISO 9000:2000

ISO 9000:2000 is the logical starting point. It begins with an explanation of the overall approach to developing a quality management system. This provides a very good overview of the subject, and part of it is reproduced in the next section of this chapter to illustrate the philosophy of ISO 9001:2000. The main part of ISO 9000:2000, however, is its comprehensive vocabulary section which contains definitions of all the terms used in ISO 9001:2000 and ISO 9004:2000. This is a very useful section and we have made use of a number of relevant definitions in this book.

2.2.2 ISO 9001:2000

ISO 9001:2000 specifies the requirements for a quality management system that can be used for certification or contractual purposes. Clearly it could also be used internally as a sound basis for managing quality without ever having your system audited or assessed by any external body. However, it is designed to facilitate assessment and is the standard to which you must demonstrate compliance if you wish to be certified by an accredited assessment body.

2.2.3 ISO 9004:2000

ISO 9004:2000 was developed to complement ISO 9001:2000. It is based on the same four major sections; management responsibility, resource management, product realisation and measurement, analysis and improvement. The sections and sub-sections have identical numbering in both standards, although ISO 9004:2000 contains much more detail than ISO 9001:2000. A helpful feature of ISO 9004:2000 is that every clause contains a separate box which shows the wording of the equivalent clause in ISO 9001:2000.

ISO 9004:2000 takes organisations beyond ISO 9001 and should be viewed more as an advisory document than as a specification. It is not intended to be used as a guideline for how to implement ISO 9001:2000 but as a source of information, ideas and advice about how the organisation can move beyond the requirements of ISO 9001:2000, especially in terms of establishing an effective continual improvement system.

The introductions to the standards also provide descriptions that help to distinguish between the three standards. The extract below comes from paragraph 03 of the Introduction to ISO 9001:2000 where the relationship with ISO 9004:2000 is described as follows:

The present editions of ISO 9001 and ISO 9004 have been developed as a consistent pair of quality management system standards which have been designed to complement each other, but can also be used independently. Although the two International Standards have different scopes, they have similar structures in order to assist their application as a consistent pair.

ISO 9001 specifies requirements for a quality management system that can be used for internal application by organisations, or for certification, or for contractual purposes. It focuses on the effectiveness of the quality management system in meeting customer requirements.

ISO 9004 gives guidance on a wider range of objectives of a quality management system than does ISO 9001, particularly for the continual improvement of an organisation's overall performance and efficiency, as well as its effectiveness. ISO 9004 is recommended as a guide for organisations whose top management wishes to move beyond the requirements of ISO 9001, in pursuit of continual improvement of performance. However, it is not intended for certification or contractual purposes.

2.3 The philosophy of ISO 9001:2000

The ISO 9001:2000 standard has made customers the focal point of a process based quality management system. Section 2 of ISO 9000:2000 covers the *Fundamentals of Quality Management Systems* and Section 2.1 explains the *Rationale for quality management systems*. The following quote from that section outlines the philosophy of the revised Standard.

Customers require products with characteristics that satisfy their needs and expectations. These needs and expectations are expressed in product specifications and collectively referred to as customer requirements. Customer requirements may be specified contractually by the customer or may be determined by the organisation itself. In either case, the customer ultimately determines the acceptability of the product. Because customer needs and expectations are changing, and because of competitive pressures and technical advances, organisations are driven to improve continually their products and processes.

The quality management system approach encourages organisations to analyse customer requirements, define the processes that contribute to the achievement of a product which is acceptable to the customer, and keep these processes under control. A quality management system can provide the framework for continual improvement to increase the profitability of enhancing customer satisfaction and the satisfaction of other interested parties. It provides confidence to the organisation and its customers that it is able to provide products that consistently fulfil requirements.

Figure 2.1, reproduced from the Standard, shows customers, not management, as the starting point of the quality management system. The role of management is '*to ensure that customer requirements are determined and are met with the aim of enhancing customer satisfaction.*' Management is also responsible for making available adequate resources to enable the organisation to develop and deliver a product (the standard uses 'product' to mean product or service), which will meet those customer requirements. To judge the organisation's success in achieving this core objective, customer satisfaction will have to be measured and the results used as a key ingredient for the continual improvement of the quality management system. This type of '*Plan-Do-Check-Act*' process is a continuous one, creating the need to identify customer requirements and measure customer satisfaction on a regular basis. ISO 9001:2000 summarises

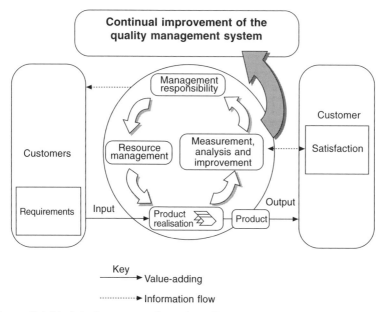

Figure 2.1 Model of a process-based quality management system

this approach right at the beginning of the Standard in Section 1.1 covering its 'Scope'.

> *This International Standard specifies requirements for a quality management system where an organisation:*
>
> (a) *Needs to demonstrate its ability to consistently provide product that meets customer and applicable regulatory requirements, and*
> (b) *Aims to enhance customer satisfaction through the effective application of the system, including processes for the continual improvement of the system and the assurance of conformity to customer and applicable regulatory requirements.*

2.4 What the Standard says

The main references of relevance to customer satisfaction measurement in the new Standard are summarised in Figure 2.2 and examined below.

Section	Requirement
ISO 9001:2000: CSM requirements	
5. Management responsibility	Top management shall ensure that customer requirements are determined and are met with the aim of enhancing customer satisfaction
6. Resource management	The organisation shall determine and provide the resources needed... (b) To enhance customer satisfaction by meeting customer requirements.
7. Product realisation	7.2.1 The organisation shall determine (a) Requirements specified by the customer . . .
8. Measurement, analysis and improvement	8.2.1 Customer satisfaction As one of the measurements of the performance of the quality management system, the organisation shall monitor information relating to customer perception as to whether the organisation has met customer requirements
8.4 Analysis of data	The organisation shall determine, collect and analyse appropriate data to demonstrate the suitability and effectiveness of the quality management system . . . The analysis of data shall provide information relating to (a) Customer satisfaction (see 8.2.1) (b) Conformity to product requirements (see 7.2.1)

Figure 2.2 A summary of references to CSM in ISO 9001:2000

2.4.1 Management responsibility

Customers are the focus of the new Standard. As we have already explained, the first section of the Standard makes it clear that the central purpose of the quality management system is to ensure that the organisation meets the needs of its customers and continually strives to enhance customer satisfaction. Section 5 places this responsibility firmly with senior management who must also ensure that adequate and appropriate resources are provided to achieve this objective.

As we will suggest in Chapter 9, conducting a customer survey will not be enough on its own to achieve the objective of continually improving customer satisfaction. Senior management must walk the talk. They must continually demonstrate their commitment to meeting customers' requirements as specified right at the beginning of the *'Management responsibility'* section in clause 5.1, *'Management commitment'*.

Top management shall provide evidence of its commitment to the development and implementation of the quality management system and continually improving its effectiveness by

(a) communicating to the organisation the importance of meeting customer as well as statutory and regulatory requirements.

Section 5.2, *'Customer focus'*, makes management responsible for the core activities of the customer satisfaction measurement process. These are developed in Sections 7 and 8 of the Standard and in Chapters 3 to 7 of this book.

Top management shall ensure that customer requirements are determined and are met with the aim of enhancing customer satisfaction (see 7.2.1 and 8.2.1).

Section 6 moves on to *'Resource management'*, where it states in clause 6.1 that:

The organisation shall determine and provide the resources needed

(a) To implement and maintain the quality management system and continually improve its effectiveness, and

(b) To enhance customer satisfaction by meeting customer requirements.

'The resources needed' for reliable customer satisfaction measurement may be greater than some organisations expect. As we will see in Chapters 3, 4 and 5, designing a questionnaire with a few colleagues, mailing it out to customers and analysing the small percentage that are returned may be a very cheap way of doing a customer survey but will not produce a reliable measure of customer satisfaction.

2.4.2 Customer requirements

As we know from the diagram shown in Figure 2.1, ISO 9001:2000 makes customers' requirements the starting point of the quality management system.

Identification of customers' requirements is found in Section 7 of the Standard covering '*Product realisation*'. Section 7.2 covers '*Customer-related processes*' and the first clause, 7.2.1, '*Determination of requirements related to the product*' addresses the need to identify customers' requirements. It states:

The organisation shall determine

(a) Requirements specified by the customer, including the requirements for delivery and post-delivery activities

(b) Requirements not stated by the customer but necessary for specified or intended use, where known

(c) Statutory and regulatory requirements related to the product, and

(d) Any additional requirements determined by the organisation.

This is not very easy to interpret. The phrase '*including the requirements for delivery and post-delivery activities*' is particularly odd since it suggests a manufacturing orientation, which the new Standard was trying to move away from. In practice, this strange wording is probably a cumbersome way of describing the 'total product', which is quite simply everything your organisation does that affects customers. This view is reinforced by ISO 9000:2000 in which clause 3.1.2 defines 'requirement' as a '*need or expectation that is stated, generally implied or obligatory*'. In other words, it could cover anything that customers regard as important.

As we will see in Chapter 3, one of the most fundamental mistakes made by organisations when introducing customer satisfaction measurement is to assume that they know what is important to their customers. All the evidence is contrary to this assumption. To be sure of correctly identifying and understanding customers' requirements, you have to consult the customers themselves. Support for this view is found in the introduction to ISO 9001:2000, paragraph 02, '*Process approach*', where the description of the diagram (Figure 2.1) states: '*This illustration shows that customers play a significant role in defining requirements as inputs.*'

2.4.3   Customer satisfaction

Section 8 of ISO 9001:2000 covers '*Measurement, analysis and improvement*'. Section 8.2 examines '*Monitoring and measurement*' and its first clause, 8.2.1, refers to '*Customer satisfaction*'. Until the latter stages of the development of the revised Standard, it seemed that organisations were to be required to do no more than monitor 'customer satisfaction or dissatisfaction'. This weak form of wording could have been addressed simply by monitoring customer complaints, leaving the situation little changed from the old Standard. Happily, this avoidance of any real obligation to satisfy customers was rectified in the final version of the new Standard. Clause 8.2.1 now specifies:

As one of the measurements of the performance of the quality management system, the organisation shall monitor information relating to customer perception as to whether the organisation has met customer requirements.

This aligns the Standard firmly with the Tom Peters view that 'perception is reality'. It is widely recognised in the customer satisfaction field that customers' perceptions do not always conform to reality. Customers have very long memories for anything that has upset them and it may take several good customer experiences to eradicate the negative attitudes arising from one bad experience. The implication of this definition is that compliance with the Standard's requirement to monitor customer satisfaction can be achieved only through asking customers about their level of satisfaction.

This view is confirmed in ISO 9000:2000, where clause 3.1.4 defines 'customer satisfaction' as:

customer's perception of the degree to which the customer's requirements have been fulfilled.

Note 1: Customer complaints are a common indicator of low customer satisfaction but their absence does not necessarily imply high customer satisfaction.

Note 2: Even when customer requirements have been agreed with the customer and fulfilled, this does not necessarily ensure high customer satisfaction.

It is certainly valid and useful to monitor customer complaints and internal measures such as delivery reliability and telephone response times, all of which will provide real time evidence of the organisation's ability to meet customers' requirements. However, the two notes in clause 3.1.4 of ISO 9000:2000 are totally correct. Lack of complaints and good organisational performance do not necessarily translate into customer satisfaction. Only an objective customer satisfaction measurement process will provide a reliable indication of how satisfied customers feel. In Chapters 4 and 5 we look at how to conduct a professional survey based on a representative sample of customers.

Section 8.4 covers *'Analysis of data'* and states:

The organisation shall determine, collect and analyse appropriate data to demonstrate the suitability and effectiveness of the quality management system and to evaluate where continual improvement of the effectiveness of the quality management system can be made. This shall include data generated as a result of monitoring and measurement and from other relevant sources.

The analysis of data shall provide information relating to

(a) Customer satisfaction (see 8.2.1)
(b) Conformity to product requirements (see 7.2.1).

Section 8.1, which provides a general introduction to *'Measurement, analysis and improvement'*, states:

> *The organisation shall plan and implement the monitoring, measurement, analysis and improvement processes needed*
>
> *(a) To demonstrate conformity of the product*
> *(b) To ensure conformity of the quality management system, and*
> *(c) To continually improve the effectiveness of the quality management system.*
>
> *This shall include determination of applicable methods, including statistical techniques, and the extent of their use.*

This suggests that the statistical techniques used for analysis of CSM data (see 8.4) could be determined by the organisation. However, for most organisations with a customer base of reasonable size, an objective quantitative survey is going to be the 'applicable method'. For organisations with a very small number of customers a more qualitative approach may be justifiable in ISO terms, but this will be a very small percentage of the market. Chapter 7 discusses how to use appropriate statistical techniques to analyse the results.

2.5 The transition to ISO 9001:2000

ISO 9001:2000 is now a live standard. Organisations seeking assessment of their quality management system for the first time can be assessed to ISO 9001:2000 with immediate effect and would be well advised to follow that course of action. Developing a new quality management system to the old standard would not be a sensible policy. Organisations who already have a system which conforms with ISO 9001:1994 or ISO 9002:1994 have a transition period during which they can continue to be assessed to their existing quality management system. The International Accreditation Forum has established a set of guidelines for Certification Bodies and this includes a maximum transition period of three years from publication of the new Standard, which was published in December 2000. However, that is the maximum time period allowed, and registered companies are strongly advised to contact their own certification body to agree a suitable transition time for their own organisation. For organisations that have not previously measured customer satisfaction, developing that capability will be one of the more challenging requirements of the new Standard. Time permitting, it would be advisable to develop and introduce a professional and reliable CSM process prior to incorporating that process into the quality management system for later assessment. It is important however, that your transition plan is agreed with your certification body.

2.6 Conclusions

(a) The first ISO quality management standard was introduced in 1987 to harmonise the many different national quality standards that had been developed.

(b) ISO 9001:2000 is supported by two complementary standards. ISO 9000:2000 provides definitions of the many terms used in the Standard and ISO 9004:2000 offers a more detailed continual improvement framework for organisations wishing to go beyond the requirements of ISO 9001:2000.

(c) Only ISO 9001:2000 can be used for certification purposes.

(d) ISO 9001:2000 has made customers the focal point of a process-based quality management system.

(e) Top management are responsible for maintaining this customer focus by ensuring that the organisation identifies and monitors its ability to meet customers' requirements.

(f) Adequate resources must be provided not just to meet customers' requirements but also to continually improve the organisation's ability to satisfy customers.

(g) Organisations certified to the 1994 version of the Standard will have until December 2003 at the latest to ensure that their quality management system complies with the requirements of ISO 9001:2000.

3

Identifying customers' requirements

Summary

The process-based approach to managing quality advocated by ISO 9001:2000 starts with customer requirements. The purpose of this chapter is to:

(a) Emphasize the importance of identifying customers' requirements.
(b) Distinguish between the lens of the customer and the lens of the organization.
(c) Explain the use of exploratory research for identifying customers' requirements.
(d) Clarify the applications of depth interviews and focus groups.
(e) Bridge the gap between identification of customers' requirements and questionnaire design.

3.1 What the Standard says

As explained in the previous chapter, one of the main principles underpinning the ISO 9000:2000 Standard is that most organisations' reason for being is to meet customers' requirements. In markets where customers have choices this has long been a basic fact of commercial life. Increasingly, however, in non-competitive situations, whether in the private or public sectors, it is recognised that organisations will not have a long-term future if they do not meet the requirements of their customers.

The Standard makes many references to 'meeting customers requirements' but provides very little explanation of precisely what 'requirements' are or how they should be identified. The key references from the Standard are:

3.1.1 ISO 9000:2000 definition

ISO 9000:2000 defines 'requirement' as *'need or expectation that is stated, generally implied or obligatory'*. The implication is that customer requirements are all embracing and that 'customer requirement' can include any factors on which customers base their judgement of your organisation. Our preferred definition is somewhat simpler:

A customer requirement is anything that is important to the customer.

3.1.2 Determining customers' requirements

Clause 7.2.1 of ISO 9001:2000 states that:

the organisation shall determine

(a) Requirements specified by the customer, including the requirements for delivery and post-delivery activities.

Combined with the ISO 9000 definition outlined above, the implication of this brief instruction is that all aspects of the organisation's activities should be covered. In other words, customers' requirements do not apply just to the core product but also to all aspects of the way in which the product is 'delivered' or provided. The word 'delivery' should not be interpreted in a narrow sense, as in physical distribution of goods, but in its broader context, covering all aspects of the supply of the product or service. However, whilst clause 7.2.1, states that the organisation must determine its customers' requirements, it does not explain how this should be done.

3.1.3 The customer's role

In fact, the Introduction to ISO 9001:2000 provides the answer. Section 02, 'Process approach', which features the continuous improvement diagram shown in Chapter 2, points firmly in the direction of customers. Its description of the diagram states:

This illustration shows that customers play a significant role in defining requirements as inputs.

As we will see later in the chapter, an accurate understanding of customers' requirements will be provided only through 'the lens of the customer', and not through 'the lens of the organisation'.

3.1.4 Whose responsibility is it?

The Standard leaves no room for doubt on this question. Section 5.2 places the responsibility for customer focus firmly with senior management. It states:

Top management shall ensure that customer requirements are determined and are met with the aim of enhancing customer satisfaction.

3.2 The importance of identifying customers' requirements

ISO 9001:2000 is based on the sound premise that meeting (or exceeding) customers' requirements is often the key ingredient of business success. The purpose of customer satisfaction measurement is to clarify the extent to which the organisation is achieving that goal. It follows therefore that to get a reliable measure of customer satisfaction you must have an accurate understanding of the customer requirements that the organisation is striving to meet. The first, and probably one of the most common mistakes that organisations make, is to assume that they do have an adequate understanding of customers' requirements. All the evidence suggests otherwise. The purpose of this chapter is to explain how to use exploratory research techniques to reliably identify customers' main requirements.

3.2.1 How *not* to do it!

Many organisations assume that designing a questionnaire for a customer survey is easy. They might arrange a meeting attended by a few managers who, between them, suggest a list of appropriate topics for the questionnaire. There are two problems with this approach. Firstly, the questionnaire almost always ends up far too long because managers tend to keep thinking of more topics on which customer feedback would be useful or interesting. The second, and more serious problem is that the questionnaire invariably covers issues of importance to the company's managers rather than those of importance to customers. This is fine if the objective is simply to understand customers' perceptions of how the organisation is performing in the specified areas, but it will not provide a measure of customer satisfaction.

3.2.2 How to do it

Think back to our original definition. The survey will provide you with a measure of satisfaction only if the questions on the questionnaire cover those things that customers were looking for in the first place. Those things that make them satisfied or dissatisfied. Therefore, if you want an accurate measure of satisfaction you have to start by going and asking the customers what their main requirements are. What are the most important things to them as customers of your organisation? Those are the topics that must be included on your questionnaire.

3.3 The lens of the customer (Figure 3.1)

In their book *Improving Customer Satisfaction, Loyalty and Profit*, Michael Johnson and Anders Gustafsson from the University of Michigan introduced

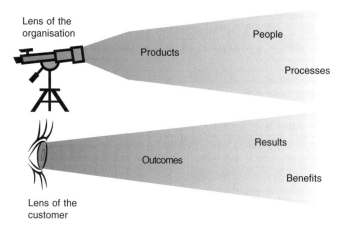

Figure 3.1 Whose perspective?

the concept of 'the lens of the customer', which they contrasted with 'the lens of the organisation'. Suppliers and their customers often do not see things in the same way. Suppliers typically think in terms of the products they supply, the people they employ to provide them and the processes that employees use to deliver the product or service. Customers look at things from their own perspective, basing their evaluation of suppliers on whether they have received the results, outcomes or benefits that they were seeking.

3.3.1 Specifications or requirements

Suppliers often formalise their 'products, people and processes' perspective into specifications and procedures. There has been a tendency for many organisations to believe that if the procedures have been followed and the specifications met, they have done all they need to do. One of the main differences between the 1994 and 2000 versions of ISO 9001 is the acknowledgement that following procedures and meeting specifications, whilst important, may not be enough to enable organisations to achieve their objectives if the end result does not satisfy customers.

Organisations are most likely to fall into the specification trap on large-scale contracts such as construction projects or supplying a new telephone system, which are often governed by detailed specifications and perhaps service level agreements. Manufactured products from cars to software are also likely to have comprehensive specifications for design and production, but adhering religiously to the specification will not necessarily result in satisfied customers if, for example, the attitude of the supplier's staff made the experience of dealing with the supplier a less than pleasant one. Scott Cook, founder of Intuit who supply Quicken personal finance software, understands this well because he views his market through the lens of the customer. Customers don't think in terms of the supplier's perspective of products, processes and people but make more subjective judgements based on the results, outcomes and benefits. So rather than just supplying reliable financial software at a good price, Intuit delivers results and benefits such as:

- Maximum 20 minute installation time from opening the box to successfully using the product.
- Lifetime free support.
- Knowledgeable helpline staff who can provide advice on tax and financial matters when necessary as well as software support.

Most customer–supplier relationships are not governed by specifications or contracts but involve a series of transactions and interactions often covering many different things. Whilst the banks may be focusing on products, people and processes, the customers are probably thinking about how quickly and easily they can get hold of cash, how flexible the bank will be if they need short-term finance, how much support they can get for investment decisions and whether their many years of loyalty will count for anything if they go temporarily overdrawn.

3.4 Exploratory research

The essential starting point for a CSM survey is therefore to carry out exploratory research to let the customers set the agenda – to highlight the main things that make them satisfied or dissatisfied. Only if the questionnaire is designed through the lens of the customer will the survey provide an accurate measurement of how satisfied customers feel. If the questionnaire is designed through the lens of the organisation, the survey will determine how well the organisation is performing in those areas it chooses to cover, but it will not measure customer satisfaction.

3.4.1 Qualitative and quantitative research

Exploratory research is qualitative research as opposed to quantitative research. Qualitative research involves getting a lot of information from a small number of customers. Lots of information is needed because at this stage you really want to understand them (in the case of CSM what's important to them as a customer), so that you can include the right questions on the questionnaire. From qualitative research you gather much information and gain a lot of understanding but since it involves only small numbers of customers it won't be statistically reliable.

Quantitative research involves getting a small amount of information from a large number of customers. In customer satisfaction measurement that happens at the main survey stage and it will be statistically reliable. In short, the qualitative (exploratory) research establishes the list of customers' main requirements enabling an accurate questionnaire to be designed. The quantitative research (main survey) establishes statistically reliable measures of customer satisfaction.

To conduct exploratory research for CSM you have to talk to some customers. You can either talk to them one at a time, so-called 'depth interviews' or in groups typically known as focus groups. We will now examine each of the exploratory research techniques in turn starting with depth interviews.

3.5 Depth interviews

Depth interviews are usually face to face and one to one. The duration of a depth interview can range from 30 to 90 minutes depending on the complexity of the customer–supplier relationship. Depth interviews are more commonly used in business-to-business markets, where the customers are other organisations so we will describe the depth interview process mainly in that context.

The first question is how many to conduct. As a generalisation, a typical number of depth interviews that would be carried out in a business market is 12. A very small customer base might need fewer. A large and complex customer base would need more but 12 would be an average number. In consumer or domestic markets a larger number of depth interviews, e.g. 30, would be normal, but focus groups would be more commonly used for exploratory research in that type of market.

3.5.1 Organising depth interviews

Since exploratory research is not statistically valid it is not necessary to use any complicated sampling techniques to select your small sample. You just use your best judgement to ensure that you have a good mix of different types of customers. If your customers are other organisations that might involve:

- a mix of high value and lower value customers;
- customers from different business sectors;
- different geographical locations;
- a range of people from the DMU (decision making unit).

This last point is an important one because if your customers are other organisations there will usually be several individuals who are affected in some way by your product or service and they will communicate with each other, formally or informally, to determine whether that customer is satisfied or dissatisfied. Your exploratory research, and later your main survey, must reach the full spectrum of these individuals if it is going to be accurate. So, for example, if your main contacts are in purchasing, don't just go and see purchasing people, go and visit some people from production, from quality, from design and any other people who might be members of the DMU.

Having decided who to visit, an appointment will have to be arranged. You therefore need to contact all the customers that you would like to interview, gain their agreement to participate and fix a convenient appointment time. You should then send a letter to all participants confirming the appointment and summarising the purpose of the interview. A typical letter of introduction for a depth interview is shown in Figure 3.2.

Depth interviews introductory letter

Dear ......

It is our intention at XYZ Inc to conduct a survey to measure the satisfaction of our customers. Prior to conducting a formal survey, we are asking a small number of customers to participate in personal interviews of approximately 1 hour in duration to clarify what is most important to you in your relationship with XYZ and how well you feel that we meet your needs in those areas. The purpose of these preliminary interviews is to ensure that our survey concentrates on issues that are relevant and important to customers.

I believe that this process needs to be carried out in a professional manner and have therefore appointed The Leadership Factor, an agency which specialises in this work, to carry out the exercise on our behalf. The work will be conducted by Mr Bill Self who will contact you in the next few days to arrange a convenient time to visit you to carry out the personal interview.

Your responses will be treated in total confidence by Mr Self and we will receive only an overall summary of the results of the interviews. Of course, if there are any particular points that you would like to draw to our attention you can ask for them to be recorded and your name associated with them if you wish.

I would like to thank you in advance for helping us with this important exercise. We will let you know the outcome and also how we plan to respond to the findings. I regard this as a very important step in our aim of continually improving the level of service we provide to our customer.

Yours sincerely

XXX XXX
President
XYZ Inc.

Figure 3.2 Sample introductory letter for depth interviews

3.5.2 Conducting depth interviews

3.5.2.1 Identifying the customer requirements

The interviewer's prime objective in a depth interview is to encourage the respondent to say as much as possible. It is therefore a good idea to start with any topic of conversation that might get the respondent talking. There might be some cues in the room (e.g. photos of football teams or a golf trophy) but in the absence of any visible prompts, a good starting point is to ask the respondent to explain his/her role in the organisation and bring that round to how he/she gets involved with your company as a customer. All of this is just an ice breaker, designed to establish rapport with the respondent before getting into the main part of the interview.

A depth interview is not a conventional interview where the interviewer asks a sequence of short questions each followed by short answers. The purpose of the depth interviews is to really understand customers, to clarify the things that are important to them, to draw out the things that make them satisfied or dissatisfied. To achieve that aim it is essential to get the respondent doing as much talking as possible. That said, it would obviously not be productive to ask closed questions – questions that can be answered with one word answers. It is better to ask open questions. But even open questions can be answered quite tersely, so it is most effective to think in terms of asking indirect rather than direct questions. An example of a direct question would be:

> *What are the things that are important to you as a customer when you're buying widgets?*

Direct questions of this nature will tend to elicit short and rather general answers, such as:

> *Well, quality's important and on time delivery, and of course price is important and service.*

To get the kind of information you need from CSM exploratory research, you need to approach the subject in a much less direct way. The same question asked in an indirect way could be something like this:

> *I'd like you to imagine that you didn't have a supplier of widgets and you had to start with a blank piece of paper and find one. I wonder if you could talk me through what would happen in this organisation from the first suggestion that you might need a supplier of widgets right through to the time when a supplier has been appointed and evaluated. As you talk me through the process, perhaps you could also point out the different people in your organisation who might get involved at different times. What sort of things would each of those people be looking for from this new supplier and what roles would they each play in the decision making process?*

This is not a question that will be answered briefly. Indeed, in some organisations it will stimulate an explanation of a very complex process that may continue for several minutes. While the respondent is talking through this process, it is useful to make two sets of notes on two pieces of paper. On the first jot down anything that seems to be important to somebody – a list of customer requirements. And on the second write down a list of all the different people that seem to be getting involved – the composition of the DMU. When the respondent has finished the explanation you can show him/her the two lists and ask if there is anything that should be added to either one.

Even though the discussion may have already taken quite some time, the respondent may not have thought of absolutely everything, so you may need to prompt them. Before starting the depth interviews, you should therefore talk to people in your own organisation and ask them what things they think are important to customers and build up a list of assumed customer requirements. Anything on that list not mentioned by the respondent should be used as a prompt. For example:

> *What about round the clock service visits, would that be of any importance to anyone in your organisation?*

If it is it should be added to the list of customer requirements. Once you have done some depth interviews, you can use as prompts anything that other customers have told you is important.

3.5.2.2 Clarifying the relative importance

After some prompting you should have generated a very comprehensive list of things that are important to the customer, and it might be a very long list. In a business market there might easily be fifty things on this list, but you cannot have as many as fifty attributes on the questionnaire for the main survey. Fifteen would be the normal number of requirements used, twenty at the most. So from this long list you need to be able to identify the things that are most important to customers. One way is to simply ask them. You could go down the list and ask them to rate each item for importance. The trouble with this approach is that virtually everything is important to customers.

Imagine you were interviewing a respondent about rail travel and had developed a long list of things that are important to him/her as a rail passenger. One of the items on the list might be '*the quality of the hot drinks from the buffet car*' – how important is that? The respondent will probably say something like:

> *It's very important. I wouldn't want weak tea, and certainly not cold tea.*

Another requirement on the list might be the punctual arrival of the train – how important is that? The respondent will probably say:

> *It's very important. Nobody wants the train to be late do they?*

If you simply ask customers to rate the importance of a list of requirements, everything will be important. But what if you ask them to compare the importance of the cup of tea and the punctual arrival of the train?

> *Which is more important, the temperature of the cup of tea or the punctual arrival of the train?*

This much more precise question will be far easier for people to answer. For most rail passengers of course, the punctual arrival of the train will be far more important. Using this 'forced trade-off' approach provides a much more accurate indication of the relative importance of a list of requirements. There are proprietary techniques which are based on it, such as Conjoint Analysis, but the problem with many of these is that they rely on making a large number of trade-offs which will get a little tedious if 50 or 70 customer requirements have been suggested! For CSM exploratory research it is therefore necessary to use a trade-off technique which will provide the required degree of accuracy but can be administered in what remains of a one hour depth interview. This is the approach we would recommend.

Start by asking the respondent to select his/her top priority by asking:

If you could only choose one thing from that list, which would be the single most important one to you as a customer?

The respondent might reply:

Punctual arrival of the train.

Then ask them to give it a score out of 10 for its importance to them, where 10 is extremely important and 1 is of no importance at all. They will almost invariably score it 10 since it is their top priority. (NB A ten-point numerical rating scale is only one of several scales which could be used. A full assessment of rating scales is provided in Chapter 5.) It is also worth asking respondents to single out the item on the list which is least important to them and to score that for importance on the same scale. The least important factor will usually, but not always, be rated 1 out of 10 for importance.

Having established a scale in the respondent's mind, you can ask him/her to score everything else for importance compared with his/her top priority of 'punctual arrival of the train'. Using this trade-off approach will provide a more accurate reflection of the relative importance of each item and will generate a far wider range of scores than simply going down the list without establishing the 'top priority' benchmark.

Once the depth interviews are completed it is a simple task to average the scores given for each requirement. Those achieving the highest average scores are the most important requirements of customers generally, and these are the items that should be included on the questionnaire for the main survey. In practice, you will often find that if you take all items averaging above 8 out of 10 for importance you will end up with about the right number of around 15–20 customer requirements for the main survey questionnaire.

It can also be enlightening to use one or two 'projective techniques' in depth interviews, but we will explore these in the context of focus groups where they are more commonly used.

3.6 Focus groups

For CSM exploratory research focus groups are similar to depth interviews, except that instead of talking to just one customer a discussion is held with six to eight customers. It is normal to run four focus groups, although more would be held for a complex customer base requiring segmentation. Where there are segments of customers who may hold very different views it is normal to segment the groups. So for example, the views of younger people and older people towards health care or pensions are likely to differ considerably. If so, it is not productive to mix them in the same focus group but better to run separate groups for younger and older customers.

3.6.1 Recruiting focus groups

Recruiting focus groups can be time consuming and difficult. Participants have to spend 90 minutes taking part in the group, typically in the evening after they have done a day's work, and they will have to travel to the venue, so you are asking quite a lot of them. Therefore focus group participants would normally be invited personally, perhaps at the point of sale, through street interviews or door to door canvassing. Telephone recruitment is also used when necessary but personal recruitment tends to result in greater respondent commitment.

It is important to provide written confirmation of all the details, such as time, location and anything respondents need to bring with them, in order to minimise the risk of any confusion arising. A sample confirmation letter is shown in Figure 3.3.

Recruiting respondents – getting their agreement to take part – is only half of the process. Ensuring that they actually attend the group is the other half, and sometimes the more difficult half. Therefore, as well as reminding people the day before, usually by telephone, it is also normal to offer them an incentive to give them an extra reason to turn out of the house on that cold winter night, instead of settling down by the fire to watch TV.

Cash is the most common incentive and rates can vary from £10 to over £50 depending on many factors. Higher rates are needed in London than the provinces and the more affluent the customer, the larger the incentive needs to be. Another critical factor is the strength of the relationship between the customer and the supplier. The weaker it is the more difficult it can be to generate any interest in or commitment to the focus groups on the part of the respondents. We were once simultaneously recruiting and running two sets of focus groups for two clients in financial services. One was in telephone banking and even with very high incentives recruitment was difficult and the attendance rate very poor. The customers had no relationship with and little commitment to the supplier. The second client was a traditional building society. Many customers had had mortgages or savings accounts over a long period, personally visited their local branch and were loyal customers. Although the topics for discussion were virtually identical for both groups the building society customers were far easier to recruit and the attendance rate was 100%.

Incentives are also used in business markets, e.g. £50 for tradespeople or shopkeepers, £100 and upwards for doctors, pharmacists or other professionals.

Confirmation letter for focus group participants

ABC Ltd: Customer discussion group

Dear

Thank you for agreeing to take part in the customer discussion group for ABC Ltd. This is an opportunity to express your views on what is important to you about (description of the service) and you can be assured that your feedback will be taken very seriously.

Your discussion group will be held on (date) at (time) at (location). A map is included to help you find the venue.

This is a genuine Market Research Project, carried out in accordance with the Market Research Society Code of Conduct, and your opinions, identity and telephone number will be kept in the strictest confidence.

The discussion will last approximately 90 minutes and you will receive £25 provided by ABC Ltd as a thank you for sparing the time and giving your views.

If you are unable to attend we would very much appreciate it if you would let us know. Please ring me (or speak to a colleague of mine) on 01484 517575.

If you wear spectacles for either close or distant work please bring them with you.

I feel sure you will enjoy the group.

Yours sincerely

Greg Roche
The Leadership Factor

Figure 3.3 Confirmation letter for focus group participants

Another alternative here is to link your focus groups with hospitality. Invite them to a football match for example and run the focus group before the match.

Focus groups are run in a wide range of venues including hotels, the supplier's own premises if suitable accommodation exists, people's homes or professional studios. The latter are fully equipped with all the technology needed to video the discussion, audio record it and, if required to view the proceedings live behind a one way mirror. It is a good idea to consider what kind of venue will make the participants feel most comfortable. It needs to be somewhere they are familiar with and somewhere they see as convenient. The local pub's function room for example, will often work better for attendance rates than the smart hotel a few miles down the road.

3.6.2 Running focus groups

Focus groups are run by a facilitator (sometimes called a moderator) who will explain the purpose of the group, ask the questions, introduce any activities and generally manage the group. The facilitator clearly needs to be an excellent communicator and an extremely good listener. He or she must also be strong enough to keep order, insist that only one participant is speaking at one time, prevent any verbose people from dominating the group and adhere to a time schedule. Since it is virtually impossible for the facilitator to take notes while all this is going on, it is normal practice to audio record groups enabling the facilitator to listen to the tapes afterwards in order to produce a summary report of the proceedings. As well as needing a high level of expertise, the facilitator must also be objective which is why it is always preferable to use a third party facilitator for focus groups, especially for CSM.

The group will often start with a few refreshments giving an opportunity for participants to chat informally to break the ice. Once the focus group starts officially, it is very important to involve everybody right at the beginning. Some people may not feel very confident in this type of situation and the longer they go without saying anything, the less likely it becomes that they ever will say anything so you need to get everyone involved at the outset. It is best to start with a couple of easy questions and literally go round the group and let everyone answer, even if you don't really need to know the answers to those particular questions.

3.6.3 Identifying customers' requirements

Once everyone has said something a CSM focus group is effectively divided into two halves. The first half is just like a typical focus group and involves the use of various techniques to encourage participants to talk about the subject, and for CSM focus groups there is just one overriding subject – what do they require as customers, what things are most important to them. Various techniques (often called projective techniques) can be used, and some are described shortly. All are designed to stimulate people to really think about the issues effectively by taking indirect questioning a stage further, prompting participants to think and talk about the issues without asking direct questions. By using these techniques you almost always get more out of the discussion.

3.6.3.1 Theme boards

One projective technique is grandly known as thematic apperception, which simply means using themes or images to uncover people's perceptions. Examples of the technique in action include asking people to draw pictures or cut pictures out of magazines which symbolise or remind them of whatever area of customer activity you are researching. It is an exercise that works well and people enjoy doing it, but it is very time consuming. Consequently what we would typically do in CSM focus groups, since we only have half the time available for projective techniques, is cut the pictures out for them, mount the pictures on boards, called theme boards, and use the theme boards as the stimulus material. There would typically be one board showing images which are positive or congruent with the brand concerned and one showing negative or incongruent images relating to the product/service in question. The focus group facilitator can then ask a very simple question such as: '*Do any of these pictures remind you of anything to do with. . .* ' (whatever the customer activity is).

3.6.3.2 Creative comparisons

A creative comparison is a projective technique that can be used in almost any exploratory research situation, depth interviews as well as focus groups, business customers as well as consumers. It is basically an analogy, comparing an organisation or product which may have few distinctive features with something else that has far more recognisable characteristics. A common example would be a question such as:

If ABC Ltd were an animal, what kind of animal would it be?

Answers may range from elephants to headless chickens, but having elicited all the animals from the group, the facilitator will ask why they thought of those particular examples. The reasons given will start to uncover participants' perceptions of the company in question. An elephant will obviously be a large company but may also be slow, trustworthy or likeable. Tigers may be used for aggressive companies or those which are fleet of foot and decisive and a fox for those who are cunning, not to be trusted, interested more in their own profits than in customers. In addition to animals, creative comparisons can be made with people such as stars from the movie or sporting worlds and even with cars, an analogy which works very well in business to business markets.

3.6.3.3 The Friendly Martian

The Friendly Martian is one of the earliest projective techniques but it is particularly applicable to CSM exploratory research. In the depth interview section we suggested that a good approach is to ask respondents to talk through the decision process in order to get some clues about which things are important to them as customers. The Friendly Martian technique is an even more indirect way of approaching that and you can use it for virtually any CSM exploratory research, with all kinds of customers in focus groups or depth interviews. Imagine you were running CSM focus groups for a restaurant. In that context, the Friendly Martian technique would be introduced as follows:

Let's imagine that a Friendly Martian (an ET-type character), came down from outer space. He's never been to the earth before, and you had to explain to this Friendly Martian how to arrange to have a meal out in a restaurant. What kind of things should he look out for, what does he need to know, what kind of things should he avoid? You've got to help this little guy to have a really good night out and make sure he doesn't end up making any mistakes. What advice would you give him?

Since the little Martian doesn't know anything, respondents will go into much more detail and mention all kinds of things that they would have taken for granted if you ask a direct question.

3.6.3.4 General discussion

As well as projective techniques, general discussion can also be very effective in uncovering issues of importance to customers. Using the restaurant example again, relevant questions that will stimulate wide ranging discussions in CSM focus groups include:

> *What kind of things make you really enjoy a meal out? What kind of things make you feel like complaining when you have a meal out?*
> *What do you like most about Restaurant XXXX? What do you like least about Restaurant XXXX?*
> *Which different restaurants have you used? How do they compare with each other? What kind of things make some better than others?*

3.6.4 Prioritising customers' requirements

Having used some of the techniques outlined above to identify a long list of things that are of some importance to customers, the remainder of the focus group needs to become much more structured. It should follow broadly the same steps that we outlined for the depth interview. First list on a flip chart all the customer requirements that have been mentioned in the discussions during the first half of the focus group. See if anybody can think of any more to add, then ask all participants to nominate their top priority and the factor that is least important and give both scores out of ten to establish clear benchmarks in their minds. This should be done on an individual basis, not collectively as a group. It is best to give out pencils and answer sheets enabling everybody to write down their individual views.

Having established everybody's top and bottom priorities each participant can read down the list and give every customer requirement a score out of ten, to denote it's relative importance compared with their benchmarks. Having completed all the groups you can work out the average scores given by all the participants and, typically, all those averaging above 8, or the top 15–20 requirements, will be used for the questionnaire for the main survey.

3.7 Conclusions

(a) ISO 9001:2000 states that organisations must identify customers' requirements.
(b) Customer requirements are basically anything that is important to customers.
(c) The only way to accurately identify customers' requirements is to consult the customers.

(d) Consulting customers through exploratory research will ensure that you use the lens of the customer rather than the lens of the organisation as the basis for your customer satisfaction survey.

(e) Depth interviews are typically used for exploratory research in business markets whilst focus groups are more common in consumer markets.

(f) Exploratory research must also clarify the relative importance of customers' requirements.

(g) The 15 to 20 most important requirements should be used for the main survey questionnaire.

4

A representative sample

Summary

Asking the right questions is the most fundamental factor that will determine the accuracy of your customer satisfaction survey. More difficult is the second prerequisite of an accurate measure, asking those questions to the right people. This is a matter of accurate sampling, and although the necessity of basing the results on a representative sample of customers is widely acknowledged, the technical aspects of doing so are little understood and often neglected. This chapter will explain the theory and practicalities of sampling in order to ensure that you produce an accurate measure by asking the right people as well as the right questions. In particular we will:

(a) Explain the difference between probability and non-probability samples.
(b) Emphasise the importance of a sample that is unbiased as well as representative.
(c) Demonstrate how to generate an unbiased and representative sample.
(d) Explain how large your sample needs to be.

4.1 What the Standard says

Section 8 of ISO 9001:2000 covers *'measurement, analysis and improvement'*. Although sampling is not specifically covered by the Standard, clause 8.1, the general introduction to the measurement section specifies that measurement, analysis and improvement activities *'shall include determination of applicable methods, including statistical techniques, and the extent of their use'*. An accurate measure of customer satisfaction will be generated only if it is based on a statistically robust sample of customers. This chapter will review the sampling methods that should be used in order to achieve that objective.

4.2 Sampling theory

In principle sampling is simple. Most organisations have a large population of customers, but to get an accurate CSM result it is not necessary to survey all of them only a relatively small sample, provided that sample is representative of the larger population. However, there are several different types of sample, as summarised in Figure 4.1.

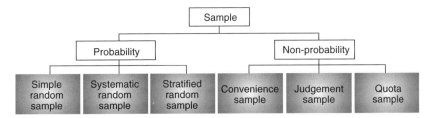

Figure 4.1 Sampling options

4.2.1 Probability and non-probability samples

The fundamental distinction between samples is whether they are probability or non-probability samples. A probability sample is often called a random sample and only a random, or probability sample, can be relied upon to be without bias. The definition of a random sample is that everybody in the population should stand an equal chance of ending up in the sample and the most obvious example of a random sample is a simple lottery. Each ball or number remaining in the lottery pool stands an equal chance of being the next ball drawn. Clearly, no element of bias can affect the selection of numbers in a lottery.

4.2.2 Non-probability samples

4.2.2.1 Convenience samples

The simplest form of sample is a convenience sample. Imagine you were doing an opinion poll. You could go into the street and ask the first 50 people you meet how satisfied they are with the performance of the Government. It would be quick, easy and cheap, but it would not be very representative. That might sound obvious, but it is very easy for apparently more sophisticated samples to degenerate into convenience samples as we'll see later.

4.2.2.2 Judgement sample

The next form of non-probability sample is a judgement or judgemental sample. That was precisely the kind of sample we suggested for the exploratory research and whilst a judgemental sample is fine for qualitative research, which does not purport to be statistically robust, it would not be suitable for the main survey or any study that has to provide a statistically reliable result.

4.2.2.3 Quota sample

The third type of non-probability sample is a quota sample and this is often used to survey large populations. Imagine that a city council wanted to measure the satisfaction of inhabitants with the facilities and services it provides. Let's assume it had decided to interview in the street a quota sample of 500 people who were resident within the city. It might appoint five interviewers to each interview 100 people in the main shopping area. However, the interviewers would not be permitted to interview a convenience sample of the first 100 people who came along. A quota sample would require each interviewer to meet a number of carefully defined quotas in order to make their sample representative of the local population. The quotas would probably be based on the population statistics held by the City Council, which would tell us how the population breaks down into groups. So for example, they might show that 15% of the population was aged 21 to 30, 18% of the population was between 31 and 40 years old and so on. There may also be other segments such as gender, income levels or ethnic groups. If the City Council wanted its sample to be representative, all those groups would have to be represented in the same proportions in the sample as they appear in the total population. To achieve this the interviewers would be set quotas. In this example, 15 of the 100 people they each interview would have to be aged 21–30, 18 would have to be aged 31–40 and these would be overlaid with quotas for the other groupings like gender, income and so on.

Let's assume that all five interviewers spent the entire working week, Monday to Friday, from 9 am to 5 pm each day interviewing in the shopping mall so that by the end of the week, they had each completed 100 interviews and met all their quotas. That would yield a sample of 500 which would be totally representative of the population of the City, but it was not randomly selected and it would not therefore be without bias. The definition of a random sample stated that everybody in the population concerned must stand an equal chance of ending up in the sample. In this example, only those people in the shopping area between 9 am and 5 pm on weekdays would stand any chance of being sampled. So it would inevitably be biased, probably towards older people, the unemployed and people who work nearby. In reality, of course, researchers try to minimise the problem of bias in quota samples by interviewing in a number of locations and at various times, but you can never eliminate it because it will remain the case that only those people in those locations at those times will stand any chance of being sampled, so, in theory, it can never be a random, and totally unbiased sample.

This does not mean that a quota sample should never be used. If you don't know who your customers are you cannot do a random sample because it is not possible to produce a list of the whole 'population' to sample from. Many retailers, for example, do not know who their customers are. They would not be able to print a list of the names of their population of customers. Organisations in that situation would typically use a quota sample.

4.2.3 Probability samples

If you have a customer database, you can and should do a random sample and the first step is to define your sampling frame. This is the list of customers that you are going to sample from and defining it is a policy decision. Typically organisations would measure customer satisfaction annually and the sampling frame would include all customers who have dealt with the organisation in the last twelve months. However, that may not be appropriate for everyone. For example, it would not be very productive for an IT help desk measuring the satisfaction of its internal customers to question a customer about his or her experience of using the help desk 11 months previously. In such circumstances it would be more normal to use a much shorter time frame, perhaps all customers using the help desk in the last month. This may necessitate continuous tracking, where customers are surveyed every month and the results are rolled up for periodic reporting, perhaps quarterly or even annually if there are not many customers.

So, as you can see, the definition of the 'customers' being surveyed may differ between different organisations and that is a policy decision but you must have a clear definition and it is those customers who will form the population for the survey, i.e. the sampling frame.

4.2.3.1 Simple random sample

A probability, or random sample will be unbiased since every member of the sampling frame will stand an equal chance of ending up in the sample. As we said earlier, a lottery is a good example of a simple random sample – each time another number is required it is randomly sampled from all those remaining in the 'population'. However, that would be a rather long process if you needed a large sample from a large population so in the days before sophisticated computer sampling market researchers invented a less time consuming way of drawing a simple random sample, strictly known as a 'systematic random sample'.

4.2.3.2 Systematic random sample

To produce a systematic random sample for a CSM survey you would first print off your list of customers. Let's say there were 1000 customers on that list and you wanted a sample of 100, which is 1 in 10 of the population. You would first generate a random number between 1 and 10. If it came out as 7, you would include in your sample the 7th name on the list, the 17th, the 27th and every 10th name thereafter, resulting in a systematic random sample of 100 customers. Before you generated that number, which was randomly generated, every customer on the list stood an equal chance of being included in the sample. So it would be a random sample, but it might not be representative, especially in a business market. This is where stratified random sampling comes in.

4.2.3.3 Stratified random sample

It is not uncommon in business markets for some customers to be much more valuable than others. Sometimes, a very large proportion of a company's business, perhaps 40 or 50% might come from the top five or six customers. With a simple or systematic random sample, it would be quite possible that not one of those top five or six customers would end up in the sample. Clearly it would not make sense to undertake a survey to measure customer satisfaction that totally ignored 40–50% of everything the business did. In a business market where most companies have a small number of high value customers and a larger number of low value customers a simple or systematic random sample will inevitably be dominated by the small customers. To achieve a sample that is representative as well as unbiased, stratified random sampling has to be used.

Producing a stratified random sample involves dividing the customers into segments or strata first and then sampling randomly within each segment. Illustrated in Figure 4.2, the sample will be representative of the customer base according to the value contributed to the business by each segment of customers. In consumer markets different segments such as age or gender may be used.

Stratified random sampling				
Value segment	% of turnover	% of sample	No. of customers	Sample fraction
High	40%	40%	40	2:1
Medium	40%	40%	160	1:2
Low	20%	20%	400	1:10

Figure 4.2 Example of a stratified random sample

4.3 A sampling example

We will work through an example of how this would be done in a typical business-to-business context. The first step in a business market is to take the database of customers and sort it in order of customer value, starting with the highest value customer and going right through to the lowest value. Then you would typically divide the list into three value segments – high value, medium value and low value customers and then sample within each segment. The process is summarised in Figure 4.2.

4.3.1 Sampling the customers

In the example shown, the company derives 40% of its turnover from its high value customers. The fundamental principle of sampling in a business market is that if a value segment accounts for 40% of turnover (or profit, or however you decide to define it), it should also make up 40% of the sample. If the company has decided to survey a sample of 200 respondents, 40% of the sample would mean that 80 respondents are required from the high value customers. There are 40 high value customers so that would mean a sampling fraction of 2:1, meaning two respondents from each customer in the high value segment. In business markets it is common practice to survey more than one respondent from the largest customers.

The medium value customers also account for 40% of turnover so they must make up 40% of the sample. That means the company needs 80 respondents from its medium value customers. Since there are 160 customers in that value segment the sampling fraction would be 1:2, meaning one respondent from every two medium value customers. This would necessitate a random sample of one in every two medium value customers. This could be easily produced using the same systematic random sampling procedure described earlier. First generate a random number between 1 and 2. Let's say it came out as 2. You would take the 2nd medium value customer on the list, the 4th, the 6th and so on.

Finally, 20% of the company's business comes from low value customers so they must make up 20% of the sample, requiring 40 respondents in this example. There are 400 low value customers, which would mean a sampling fraction of 1:10. This could be produced using the same systematic random sampling procedure. By the end of the process the company would have produced a stratified random sample of customers that was representative of its business and, due to its random selection would also be without bias.

4.3.2 Sampling the contacts

Although the procedure described above has produced a random and representative sample of customers, surveys are not completed by companies but by individuals, so if you operate in a business-to-business market you will have to sample the individual contacts as well as the customers. In practice, organisations often choose the individuals on the basis of convenience – the people with whom they have most contact, whose names are readily to hand. If the individuals are selected on this basis it would mean that however carefully a stratified random sample of companies had been produced, at the 11th hour it has degenerated into a convenience sample of individuals whom somebody knows. To avoid that intrusion of bias you should randomly sample the individuals. Compiling a list of individuals who are affected by your product or service at each customer in the sample and then selecting the individuals randomly from that list is the way to do this. If you want to add complication, but also accuracy, you should stratify the list of individuals to avoid getting too many peripheral ones. For example, you might analyse the DMU and decide that to accurately reflect the decision making process your sample should be made up of 40% purchasing contacts, 40% technical contacts and 20% from all other types of contact. If so you should randomly sample the individuals in those proportions.

4.4 Sample size

The next question to tackle is the number of customers that you need in the sample. Some companies, typically in business-to-business markets, have a very small number of high value accounts. Other companies have over a million customers. In a business market the size of the population is actually the number of individuals in each customer who influence the satisfaction judgement of that customer – and that is not necessarily the same thing as the number of individuals that you have regular contact with. Typically, the higher value the customer the more individuals will be involved. For a computer software supplier, there may be several hundred users at one customer site. Even so, some organisations will have much larger populations than others, but this will not affect the number of customers they need to survey for a reliable sample.

4.4.1 Sample reliability relates to sample size

Statistically the accuracy of a sample is based on the absolute size of the sample regardless of how many people are in the total population. Asking what proportion of customers should be surveyed is not a relevant question. A larger sample will always be more reliable than a smaller sample whatever the size of the total population. This is best demonstrated by the normal distribution curve (see Figure 4.3), which basically tells us that whenever we examine a set of data it tends to follow this normal distribution. It does not apply only to research data. We might, for example, be looking at the average rainfall in Manchester in June over the last 300 years. We might see that in some years there has been virtually no rainfall in June (even in Manchester), for a few years there has been an incredibly high rainfall, but for most years the rainfall in June falls somewhere between those extremes in the 'normal' zone. Whether we are looking at data from a research survey or rain in Manchester, the key question is this – 'What is the risk of abnormal data skewing the overall result?' The smaller the sample, the greater the risk.

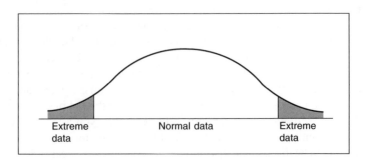

Figure 4.3 Normal distribution curve

For example, if you recorded the rainfall in June in Manchester over a five-year period when three of the years experienced normal June rainfall but two had exceptionally wet Junes, the average rainfall calculation would be heavily skewed by the two unseasonably wet months. If the data had been collected over 100 years, two exceptionally wet or dry months would make little impact on the overall result for the average rainfall in June in Manchester. The principle is the same with surveys. If you survey only 10 people and two of them happen to hold extreme views they would skew the overall result very heavily. They would make much less impact on a sample size of 50 and virtually no impact on a sample of 500, so the larger the sample the lower the risk of getting a rogue result. Figure 4.4 shows that as the sample size increases, so does its reliability. At first, with very small sample sizes the reliability increases very steeply, but as the sample size grows there are diminishing returns in terms of reliability from any further increases in sample size. You can see that the curve starts to flatten in the 30 to 50 respondents zone, and this is typically said to be the threshold between qualitative and quantitative studies. By the time the sample size has reached 200, the gains in reliability from increasing the number of respondents in the sample are very small. Consequently, a sample size of 200 is widely considered to be the minimum sample size overall for adequate reliability for CSM. Companies with a very small customer base (around or below 200 contacts) should simply carry out a census survey.

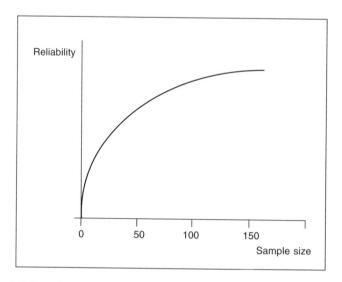

Figure 4.4 Sample size and reliability

4.4.2 Drilling down

As stated earlier, it is generally held in commercial research that a sample of 200 gives you adequate reliability for an overall measure of customer satisfaction whether you have a population of 500 or 500 000. However, there is one major exception, and that arises if you have various segments and you want to drill down into the results to compare in the satisfaction levels of various segments. If you divide a sample of 200 into many segments you will end up with the problem of small and therefore unreliable sample sizes for each segment. Therefore, it is generally accepted that the minimum overall sample size is 200 and the minimum per segment is 50.

As a consequence your total sample size will often be determined by how many segments you want to drill down into. If you want to divide your result into six segments you would need a sample of at least 300 to get 50 in every segment. This can have a major impact for companies with multiple branches or outlets. On the basis of 50 per segment, a retailer with 100 stores would need a minimum sample of 5000 if customer satisfaction is to be measured at store level. However, our view is that if comparisons are to be made between stores and management decisions taken on the basis of the results, an absolute minimum of 100 customers per store should be surveyed and preferably 200. For a retailer with 100 stores, this would result in a total sample size of 20 000 customers for a very reliable result at store level.

4.4.3 Sample size and response rates

There is one additional point to make here. The recommended sample size of 200 for adequate reliability means responses and not the number of customers sampled and invited to participate. Moreover, for statistical reliability, it means 200 customers sampled and the same 200 participating – completing the interview or returning the questionnaires. If the response rate is low, it is not reliable statistically to compensate by simply sending more questionnaires out until you have achieved 200 responses. The problem of 'non-response bias' can be a considerable one in CSM studies and will be explored in more detail in the next chapter.

4.5 Conclusions

(a) ISO 9000:2000 suggests that recognised statistical methods should be used to generate a reliable sample for customer measurements.
(b) Non-probability samples increase the risk of a biased result and should be used only by organisations with no customer database.
(c) For most organisations, stratified random sampling will be the best way to generate a sample that is both unbiased and representative.
(d) Sampling should be based on a sampling frame comprising relevant individuals. In business this could involve a number of respondents (occasionally a large number) from large customers.
(d) 200 responses is the minimum number for a reliable measure of customer satisfaction at the overall level. This applies regardless of how many customers you have.

(e) Organisations with fewer than 200 customers or contacts should conduct a census survey.
(f) If the results are to be broken down into segments, the minimum sample size per segment should be 50 respondents. In such cases the required sample size will be the number of segments multiplied by 50.

5

Survey decisions

Summary

We have now covered the two main elements that will determine the accuracy of your measure of customer satisfaction – asking the right questions to the right people. You are now ready to start on the main survey. However, before you can finalise the questionnaire design and conduct the survey, you do need to consider what type of survey would be most appropriate and this is the topic we will address in this chapter. The aims of this chapter are to:

(a) Analyse the advantages and disadvantages of the three main methods of data collection; personal interviews, telephone interviews and self-completion questionnaires in order to help you decide which is most suitable for your organisation.
(b) Provide guidance on how to maximise response rates.
(c) Understand the role of new technology such as web and e-mail surveys.
(d) Explain the advantages and risks of mixing survey types.
(e) Consider the question of respondent confidentiality and how that might affect the results of your survey.
(f) Explain when and how often to survey customers.

5.1 What the Standard says

The main references to measuring customer satisfaction are found in Section 8, 'Measurement, analysis and improvement' and particularly in paragraph 8.2, 'Monitoring and measurement'. The first clause, 8.2.1, is entitled 'Customer satisfaction' and states:

> As one of the measurements of the performance of the quality management system, the organisation shall monitor information relating to customer perception as to whether the organisation has met customer requirements. The methods for obtaining and using this information shall be determined.

A key indicator is the use of the phrase 'customer perception'. This means that it is the customer's perception of what has been provided, rather than the reality that counts. This can sometimes be frustrating for organisations when customers' perceptions do not align with reality, a so-called 'perception gap', and this situation can occur for a number of reasons. A common example is when an organisation makes improvements in an area where quality has been poor. British Leyland cars developed a reputation for poor reliability in the 1970s and early 1980s. Quality was improved considerably under Michael Edwardes and Graham Day, but it took some years (and a change of name to Rover) for customer perception to catch up with the reality of Rover's improved quality levels. It is widely acknowledged that customers notice and remember poor quality but tend to take good quality for granted. Worse still, they will often tell many other people about a bad customer experience. This demonstrates why it is so important to monitor customers' perception of quality as well as to monitor the real levels of quality delivered by the organisation. In the real world of business customer perception is reality. Customers make choices in the market based on their perception of the relative quality and value offered by competing suppliers. If their perceptions are wrong, the only sensible course of action for the injured supplier is to redouble efforts to modify customers' perceptions. This may involve tangible demonstration of superior value by delivering superb levels of quality and service, which will typically be supported by very strong communications to reinforce that value proposition. When a 'perception gap' does exist, organisations will understand their disappointing sales or falling market share only if they have an accurate measure of *'customer perception as to whether the organisation has met customer requirements.'* There is only one way to develop that knowledge. You have to ask the customers. This chapter is about how that should be done.

ISO 9001:2000 is not very helpful on this matter. As we have seen above, Section 8.1 simply states that *'the methods for obtaining and using this information shall be determined'*. However, paragraph 8.1, which is a general introduction to the 'Measurement, analysis and improvement' section does provide some more clues. It states:

The organisation shall plan and implement the monitoring, measurement, analysis and improvement processes needed

(a) To demonstrate conformity of the product
(b) To ensure conformity of the quality management system, and
(c) To continually improve the effectiveness of the quality management system.

This shall include determination of applicable methods, including statistical techniques, and the extent of their use.

This suggests that the statistical techniques used for analysis of CSM data could be determined by the organisation. However, for most organisations with a customer base of reasonable size, an objective quantitative survey is going to be the 'applicable method'. Only a quantitative survey based on a robust sample will provide a reliable guide to *'customer perception as to whether the organisation has met customer requirements'*. Even for organisations with a very small number of customers a quantitative survey is advisable since each of those customers is likely to have a DMU of some considerable size, and it is the individuals in the DMU, not the customer organisations, which must be surveyed. We have experience of interviewing as many as 50 individuals from one customer organisation, albeit a very large one. So for a reliable measure of customer satisfaction, even organisations whose customer base comprises a small number of key accounts should conduct a quantitative survey, probably with a census of contacts from within those accounts. (Regardless of the number of accounts, if your total number of contacts is below 200 a census of contacts would be appropriate.) The first step therefore is to decide what kind of survey will be undertaken, in other words, how the data will be collected.

5.2 Personal interviews

Personal interviews involve interviewing customers face to face but can take many forms.

- Exit interviews are conducted as people complete their customer experience. Customers can be surveyed as they leave a shop, finish their meal in a restaurant or check out of a hotel.
- Customers can also be interviewed during their customer experience. This can be very cost-effective if customers have time on their hands, such as waiting at an airport or travelling on a train.
- In-home interviews are convenient for consumers.
- Business customers can be interviewed at work at a time convenient to them.
- Street interviews can be used in situations where a large part of the population falls within the target group.

Whilst the most common method of personal interviewing involves writing the respondents' answers onto paper questionnaires, there are alternatives. If speed is vital, computer assisted personal interviews (CAPI) can be used. Interviewers are provided with palm top computers from which responses can be downloaded daily. With enough interviewers, a large survey can be conducted within days. Long interviews (typically in the home or the office) can be recorded so that the detail of customer comments can be captured more efficiently. However, although appropriate for depth interviews at the exploratory stage, this is not a common occurrence at the quantitative stage of customer satisfaction surveys. At this stage, interviews will usually be short (typically 10 minutes and no more than 20), and most questions will be closed. To decide whether personal interviews of customers would be appropriate for your organisation, you need to consider their advantages and disadvantages.

5.2.1 Personal interviews – advantages

Personal interviews have a number of important advantages:

- It is easier to build rapport with the respondent in the face-to-face situation.
- It is much easier to achieve total respondent understanding. Not only can things be explained but also with face-to-face interviews it is usually possible to see if the respondent is having a problem with the question.
- Visual prompts such as cards and diagrams can be used, to visibly demonstrate the range of responses on a rating scale for example.
- Complex questions become more feasible because they can be more easily explained.
- Personal interviews can be very cost-effective with a captive audience, such as passengers on a train, spectators at a sporting event or shoppers in a busy store, because where there are plenty of people in one place it is often possible to conduct large numbers of interviews in a short space of time.
- It is usually possible to gather a good deal of qualitative information in addition to the straight scores because the interviewer can establish rapport with the respondents who become more talkative as a result.
- In some situations, such as visiting people at home or at their place of work, it is feasible to conduct quite long interviews, up to half an hour, allowing plenty of time to explore issues in some depth.

5.2.2 Personal interviews – disadvantages

There are disadvantages to personal interviews, mainly relating to the cost.

- Personal interviews will usually be the most costly data collection option.
- For customer satisfaction surveys in business-to-business markets you need high calibre 'executive' interviewers who can hold a conversation at the same level as the people they are interviewing. In business markets the respondents will usually be senior people who will soon become irritated and often alienated from the process if they feel that the interviewer does not fully understand the topics under discussion.
- Customers are often scattered over a wide geographical area so more time can be spent travelling than interviewing. It is not unusual in business-to-business markets to average no more than two personal interviews per day. As well as the time involved, the travel itself is likely to be costly.
- Since many people do not like to give offence (by giving low satisfaction scores for example), there may be a tendency to be less frank in the face-to-face situation, especially if the interviewer is employed by or associated with the organisation conducting the survey.

5.3 Telephone interviews

A second data collection option involves interviewing customers by telephone, typically at work in business markets and at home in consumer markets. Responses can be recorded on paper questionnaires or, using computer assisted telephone interviews (CATI), data can be captured straight onto the computer. Let's consider the advantages and disadvantages of telephone interviews.

5.3.1 Telephone interviews – advantages

- Telephone interviews are usually the quickest controllable way of gathering survey data.
- They are relatively low cost and normally much less costly than personal interviews.
- The two-way communication means that the interviewer can still explain things and minimise the risk of misunderstanding.
- It is possible to gather reasonable amounts of qualitative information in order to understand the reasons underlying the scores. For example, interviewers can be given an instruction to probe any satisfaction scores below a certain level to ensure that the survey identifies why customers are dissatisfied and not just that they are dissatisfied.
- Distance is not a problem even in worldwide markets.

5.3.2 Telephone interviews – disadvantages

- Interviews have to be short. Ten minutes is enough for a telephone interview especially when interviewing consumers at home in the evenings. Up to 15 minutes is acceptable for business interviews during the day.
- Questions have to be quite short and straightforward. As we will see when we look at rating scales in Chapter 6, there are certain types of question that cannot be used on the telephone.
- One of the biggest frustrations with telephone surveys is that people do not seem to be sitting on the other end of the telephone waiting to be interviewed! You have to be prepared to make multiple call-backs to get a reliable sample, as shown by the statistics in Figure 5.1.

In household markets the hit rate tends to be better than the figures shown in the table but in business markets it can easily be worse. For that reason it would be good practice to make up to five call-backs for domestic interviews and up to eight in business markets to ensure good sampling reliability.

- Telephone surveys require good interviewers. For all interviews they need to be sufficiently authoritative to persuade respondents to participate and sufficiently relaxed and friendly to build rapport. As with personal interviews,

Average number of attempts required to make contact in telephone surveys			
1	attempt reaches	24%	of the sample
5	attempts reach	75%	of the sample
8	attempts reach	89%	of the sample
17	attempts reach	100%	of the sample

Figure 5.1 Multiple call-backs for accurate sampling

telephone interviews in business markets need 'executive' interviewers of high calibre who can communicate at the same level as the respondent.

5.4 Self-completion questionnaires

Self-completion questionnaires are usually administered in the form of a postal survey, although other methods of distribution such as fax, e-mail or point of sale questionnaires can be used. Whatever the distribution method, self-completion questionnaires are filled in alone by respondents without help from a researcher. They have a number of advantages and disadvantages.

5.4.1 Self-completion questionnaires – advantages

- Self-completion questionnaires will usually be the cheapest method of data collection for most surveys. However, there are many hidden costs such as handling and printing which boost the real cost of postal surveys.
- There is clearly no risk of interviewer bias.
- Most respondents will see a self-completion questionnaire as the least intrusive way of being surveyed.
- Anonymity can also be easier to guarantee on self-completion questionnaires although this will be compromised by anything printed on the questionnaire that looks as though it could be a personal identification code. Many people also mistrust the anonymity of web and e-mail surveys.
- Self-completion questionnaires are ideally suited to surveys of internal customers. They are very low cost and it is easier to implement policies to ensure a good response rate.
- For similar reasons, self-completion questionnaires are also good at the point of sale immediately after the 'customer experience'.

5.4.2 Self-completion questionnaires – disadvantages

- Postal surveys are very slow. Without a clear deadline for responses, some questionnaires will come back weeks after they were mailed out.
- Response rates tend to be low, sometimes less than 10% although they can vary enormously.
- Questionnaires have to be short.
- Questions have to be simple. People will tend to make a quick judgement about the time it will take to complete the questionnaire, and that will be a combination of the questionnaire's length and its perceived difficulty. Moreover, since questions cannot be explained to respondents, they do have to be very straightforward. An obvious factor here is the wide variation in people's reading abilities.
- One of the biggest disadvantages of most forms of self-completion survey is that as soon as you send it out you immediately abdicate control. You lose control over who fills it in and how it is filled in. You may have a painstakingly constructed sample of key decision makers who receive the questionnaire and immediately pass it to a subordinate to complete. You also have no control or knowledge of how they fill it in – whether they rush it and give it very little thought, and even whether they understand the questions or the instructions. If there are any grounds for suspicion that a questionnaire has been incorrectly completed it should be discarded as invalid.
- By far the main disadvantage of self-completion questionnaires, however, is the problem of unrepresentative samples. If a self-completion questionnaire achieves a response rate of 20%, is it possible to say that the views expressed by the 20% who returned the questionnaire are the same as the views held by the 80% who did not? In fact, it has been demonstrated by tests that self-completion surveys with low response rates suffer from the problem of 'non-response bias'. Some forms of bias, such as demographic bias, can be corrected. For example, a survey of householders is more likely to be returned by retired people than by busy parents who both have careers. This type of age-related bias could be corrected at the analysis stage but it is not possible to correct attitude bias. Tests demonstrate that non-response bias is often an attitude problem, with customers at the extremes of the normal distribution curve over-represented. In other words the most satisfied customers complete the questionnaire as an act of loyalty as does anybody who sees it as a convenient medium for grumbling, moaning and complaining. The problem is that you just do not know what the other 80% think and without surveying them there is no way of finding out!

5.5 Maximising response rates

Probably the most common question that we are asked when presenting our seminar on Customer Satisfaction Measurement is how to improve response rates on postal surveys. For anybody aiming to use this approach to measure customer satisfaction it is a vital question since the problem of non-response bias can invalidate the whole exercise if the response rate is low. Moreover, you should not forget the point of the exercise. Measuring customer satisfaction is not just a matter of carrying out a customer survey, asking a few questions and getting some feedback. It is meant to be a measure, usually one that is monitored over time as a key indicator of organisational performance, so an inaccurate measure is worse than no measure at all.

The generally accepted figure for an 'average' response rate for customer satisfaction surveys by post is 25%, but this masks an extremely wide variation from below 10% to over 90%. Typically, the more important the topic is to the customer, the higher will be the base response rate. For example, a satisfaction survey of new car buyers is likely to generate a higher response rate than a survey by a utility company. In business markets customers are more likely to complete a survey for a major supplier than a peripheral one. For customer satisfaction surveys by post, the average response rate is 25% although it is typically rather higher with business customers and lower with householders.

A response rate below 50% cannot be relied on to provide an accurate measure of customer satisfaction. You need to get over 50%, which is a very tall order in some markets. However, due to the high level of interest in response rates, quite a large body of knowledge now exists on the subject. Techniques to boost response rates can be divided into four categories:

- Essentials
- Advisables
- Marginals
- Avoidables

5.5.1 Essentials

There are some things that are essential to achieving an adequate response rate. They include:

- accurate database;
- reply paid envelope;
- follow-up strategy;
- introductory letter.

5.5.1.1 Accurate database

The most important essential, especially in business markets, is an accurate, up to date database including contact names and correct job titles. The accuracy of business databases can erode by 30% annually so you can soon be mailing lots of incorrectly addressed questionnaires.

5.5.1.2 Reply paid envelope

Respondents now expect a postage paid reply envelope and all research studies show a significantly reduced response rate if it is omitted. Some people are tempted to try fax-back questionnaires in business markets on the grounds that it might be easier for respondents to simply pop it in the fax machine. Tests show this assumption to be mistaken. Many people in large offices do not have easy access to a fax machine. Therefore, by all means include a fax-back option and a prominent return fax number, but include a reply paid envelope as well.

5.5.1.3 Follow-up strategy

A follow-up strategy is also widely endorsed by the research studies. The word strategy is important because more than one reminder will continue to generate additional responses, albeit with diminishing returns. A multiple follow-up strategy has been widely reported to have a positive effect on response rates. The more intensive the follow-up strategy the better the results. The ultimate follow-up strategy involves a four-step approach, as shown in Figure 5.2.

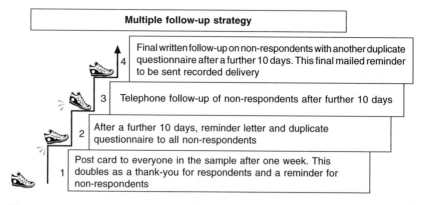

Multiple follow-up strategy

4 — Final written follow-up on non-respondents with another duplicate questionnaire after a further 10 days. This final mailed reminder to be sent recorded delivery

3 — Telephone follow-up of non-respondents after further 10 days

2 — After a further 10 days, reminder letter and duplicate questionnaire to all non-respondents

1 — Post card to everyone in the sample after one week. This doubles as a thank-you for respondents and a reminder for non-respondents

Figure 5.2 Multiple follow-up strategy

This intensive follow-up strategy can more than double response rates with as much as 83% being achieved in experiments. The obvious disadvantages are the time and cost involved, although as the cost of the follow-up steps increases there should be fewer non-respondents left to chase. Secondly, the system does rely on the ability to identify respondents, so unless the replies are sent to a neutral third party it will have a negative effect on the perceived confidentiality of the exercise.

5.5.1.4 Introductory letter

For customer satisfaction surveys, the introductory letter accompanying the questionnaire is likely to be more effective than any single step of the follow-up strategy. It should concentrate on explaining why it is in the respondent's own interest to complete the questionnaire. This is supported by several studies showing significantly higher response rates when respondents are interested in the aims and outcomes of the research compared with less specific surveys aimed at the general public. Academic tests have also shown that covering letters offering feedback on the results have a significant positive impact on response rates. Our experience supports this, especially in business markets. In our view a good covering letter highlighting benefits to respondents and promising feedback will boost response rates by around 30% on average. Both the introductory letter and post-survey feedback to customers will be covered in more detail later in this book.

5.5.2 Advisables

Three more measures that are generally agreed to boost response rates, although by a lower margin are:

✓ Pre-notification
✓ Questionnaire design
✓ Money

5.5.2.1 Pre-notification

The effectiveness of pre-notification has been shown by several academic studies. Their conclusion is that pre-notification almost always works, with telephone pre-notification the most costly but most effective method (doubling response rates in some studies). Mail pre-notification has a small but positive effect in consumer markets but the research is inconclusive for business markets, although our own experience demonstrates a strong effect when pre-notification letters are sent to business customers for telephone surveys. For postal surveys in business markets we advise sending the introductory letter with the questionnaire, supported where feasible by personal pre-notification from sales people. A recent innovation, suitable only for large companies with many customers and big budgets, has been the use of mass communications media such as TV advertising to notify people of a forthcoming survey and its benefits to customers.

5.5.2.2 Questionnaire design

Questionnaire design, rather than length, is a significant factor. If respondents' initial impression is that the questionnaire will be difficult to complete the response rate will be depressed. Academic research shows that apart from very long questionnaires, length is a less significant factor, so it is better to have clear instructions and a spacious layout spreading to four sides of paper, rather than a cluttered two-page questionnaire. More specifically, research suggests that it makes no difference to response rates whether people are asked to check boxes or circle numbers/words, nor whether space is included for additional comments.

5.5.2.3 Money

Money also seems to be a motivator! Not incentives generally but money specifically. And money now! Research in the USA has shown that a quite modest monetary reward, such as $1 attached to the introductory letter will have a significant effect in business as well as domestic markets. However, it is important that the money goes with the questionnaire. Future promises of payment to respondents are less effective and 'birds in the bush' such as prize draws, much less effective. Some people rather scurrilously suggest that researchers can reduce costs by enclosing money only with the first reminder, a tactic you might get away with if you have a sample of individuals who are unlikely to communicate with each other!

5.5.3 Marginals

The evidence for some response boosting techniques is much more equivocal. These include:

? Use of colour
? Postage rate
? Anonymity

5.5.3.1 Use of colour

The use of colour is a contentious issue. Some people advocate the use of coloured envelopes or the printing of relevant messages on envelopes. However, it is generally accepted that 10% of direct mailings are rejected without opening, so if your envelope suggests junk mail you are likely to depress the number of responses by 10%. Sticky address labels are also associated with direct mail so we advise using plain white window envelopes.

Use of colour on the questionnaires should also be considered. It is generally accepted that the use of more than one colour for printing the questionnaire will enhance clarity of layout, ease of completion and general attractiveness of the questionnaire and will therefore boost response rates. Claims have been made for printing the questionnaire on coloured paper on the grounds that it is more conspicuous to people who put it on one side, intending to complete it in a spare moment. However, a very large split test by Cranfield University and the Manchester Business School in 1997 demonstrated that there is nothing to be gained from using coloured paper on questionnaires. In fact, in their test, the questionnaires on white paper achieved slightly higher response rates.

5.5.3.2 Postage rate

There is some evidence from academic research that the use of first class mail for mail out and reply envelopes will help response rates slightly. The type of stamp used is also an issue. The use of a real stamp rather than a franking machine or a mailsort stamp will help response rates as the latter are associated with direct mail.

5.5.3.3 Anonymity

It is conventional wisdom that response rates and accuracy will be higher where respondents are confident of anonymity and confidentiality. Practitioner evidence strongly supports this view for employee satisfaction surveys and most types of satisfaction surveys in business markets, where the respondent foresees an ongoing personal relationship with the supplier. In mass markets where personal relationships are normally absent there is no conclusive evidence that anonymity increases response although in potentially sensitive areas such as financial services anonymity is preferable. Of course, there is a trade-off here with follow-up strategies, which will be much more cost-effective if respondents are required to identify themselves. In many consumer markets it may therefore be better to ask respondents to identify themselves in order to improve the cost-effectiveness of follow-up strategies.

5.5.4 Avoidables

There are some frequently used response-boosting techniques that are eminently avoidable since there is no conclusive evidence that they consistently improve response rates. Indeed, they may reduce quality of response and they are usually costly. Mainly concerning various types of incentive, avoidables include:

- Prize draws
- Free gift
- Coupons
- Donations to charity

5.5.4.1 Incentives

Research carried out in the USA suggests that the chance of future monetary reward, such as a prize draw, makes no difference unless it is very large. Also in America, academic tests report no effect from the promise of a donation to charity. Recent research in the UK suggests that the inclusion of discount coupons can even depress response rates, perhaps because they give the impression that the survey is sales driven. Even increasing the value of coupons has no effect, suggesting that redeemable discount coupons are not seen as being monetary in nature. Perhaps more surprisingly tests also show that the inclusion of a free gift (other than money) does not boost and may reduce response rates presumably because of its association with mass mailings.

5.5.5 Maximising response rates – a summary

Based on academic research, plus our own experience and that of other practitioners, Figure 5.3 indicates the average effect on response rates of the measures reviewed in this chapter. The chart assumes a reasonable questionnaire, personally addressed, mailed to the correct address and including a postage paid reply envelope. It suggests the likely increase in your base response rate. For example, a 20% improvement on a 30% response rate would result in a 36% response rate. For customer satisfaction surveys average base response rates are typically below 20% in mass markets and around 30% in closer relationship business markets.

- The most effective way of increasing response is the inclusion of a good introductory letter that spells out why it is in the customer's interest to return the questionnaire. On average this will improve the base response rate by 30%.
- Sending a postal reminder will improve response by a further 25%. This should be done ten days after the original mailing with a further copy of the questionnaire included in the letter.
- After another ten days a telephone reminder would yield a further 25% improvement.
- A user-friendly questionnaire, not too long, attractively designed and with a couple of easy questions at the beginning can add another 20%.
- An advance notice letter, sent a few days before the survey, can achieve a further 15% since it conditions respondents to expect the questionnaire.
- Many people mistakenly assume that an incentive is the best way to improve response rates. A large number of tests show that this is not the case. It is therefore more sensible to focus more attention on the alternative ways of increasing response, which, in the main, are less costly and more effective.

Techniques for maximising response rates	
Introductory letter	30%
First reminder letter	25%
Telephone reminder	25%
Respondent friendly questionnaire	20%
Advance notice letter	15%
Incentive	< 15%
Second reminder letter	12%
Envelope	+/– 10%

Figure 5.3 Techniques for maximising response rates

- Even a second reminder letter can achieve a further 12%, which is more than most incentives.
- Heavily over-printed envelopes are usually associated with direct mailings, 10% of which are rejected without being opened. To avoid this risk it is preferable to send postal questionnaires in plain, personally addressed envelopes, which will at least be opened.

As we said earlier, low response rates pose a very serious threat to the reliability of the data generated by customer satisfaction surveys due to the problem of non-response bias. The risk is increasing as people in their work and private lives suffer growing time pressure. Many people work on the mistaken principle that to increase the reliability of postal surveys with disappointing response rates they simply need to send more questionnaires out in order to get more back. This is totally mistaken. The problem is not the size of the response but the response rate. Only by improving the response rate can you overcome the problem of non-response bias.

If you want an accurate measure of customer satisfaction non-response bias is clearly a fundamental problem. For some surveys it casts a serious doubt over the acceptability of postal surveys. If you need a 50% response rate for adequate reliability you either have to work very hard to maximise the response rate or opt for a method of data collection such as telephone where that level of response will be much more easily achievable.

5.6 New technology

Interest in the use of new technology for conducting research typically focuses on the web but there are also applications in telephone research.

5.6.1 Web surveys

Although both use the internet, we should initially distinguish web from e-mail surveys. An e-mail survey involves sending questionnaires to customers by e-mail, typically in the form of a file attachment. The customer opens the file attachment, completes the questionnaire and returns it to the sender. A web survey would be completed by logging onto a web site and is usually preferable to an e-mail survey since it avoids the software problems that can be experienced with file attachments. However, in business markets it should be borne in mind that some people may be authorised to use e-mail but not the internet. There is evidence that response to e-mail and web surveys is quicker than for other types of self-completion survey but no evidence that response rates are higher. Web surveys, typically in the form of exit surveys, are useful for e-commerce businesses, especially for measuring satisfaction with the web site itself. However, even for e-commerce businesses that should not be confused with a full measure of customer satisfaction since it would precede order fulfilment and ignore any requirement for after sales service. For a worthwhile measure of customer satisfaction, e-businesses should invite a random sample of customers to complete a web survey that covers all customer requirements. Even then, a web survey with a low response rate will suffer from non-response bias in the same way as a postal survey.

For most organisations, however, there are two problems with web or e-mail surveys.

- Sampling
  Regardless of response rates, it remains impossible for most businesses even to generate a representative sample for web or e-mail surveys since many of their customers are not active web or e-mail users. This problem is diminishing all the time but it is unlikely to disappear in the short term, even in the USA.
- Confidentiality
  People are very suspicious about confidentiality on web or e-mail surveys. This will be reduced, but not eliminated, by using an objective third party as the reply e-mail address or the host of the web survey. We know of many cases where response rates have significantly reduced when the survey became electronic. Interestingly, the most suspicious respondents are IT specialists.

Technically there are few problems to conducting web or e-mail surveys. Software for both is readily available and data from responses is easily downloadable into all common types of analytical software. Questionnaire design is the most critical technical requirement since respondents will readily abort if they experience problems with completing the questionnaire.

5.6.2 Interactive voice response

Interactive voice response (IVR) enables respondents to use a touch-tone telephone to answer a series of multiple-choice questions. People would typically be invited to dial a toll free number following which a pre-recorded script administers the questionnaire. Since there is no human being at the other end of the telephone the cost per interview is very low, but there is no opportunity to seek clarification or engage in dialogue of any kind. The initial programming is also time consuming so cost saving relies on a large sample. IVR can be very cost-effective for applications such as the initial screening of job applicants. In this situation people are highly motivated to make the initial call and scripts are usually very simple, involving a few screening questions and the collection of basic information. There are three main problems associated with using IVR to generate a reliable measure of customer satisfaction.

- Sampling
  Since participation is purely voluntary the sample will be a convenience sample and response rates for surveys will usually be low.

- Unfriendliness
  Most people do not like IVR. It will be seen as the most impersonal way of collecting survey data, even more so than postal or web surveys, since personal interaction is not expected with these media. The uncaring image of IVR will also make some respondents feel that the organisation is not really interested in its customers.
- Questionnaire design
  Many customer satisfaction questionnaires can be quite complex and IVR is most appropriate for simple, short scripts.

5.7 Choosing the most appropriate type of survey

5.7.1 Telephone or postal

Most organisations will reject the personal interview option because of cost and web surveys due to the impossibility of achieving a reliable sample. Therefore, the choice for most organisations will be between a telephone and a postal survey. The postal option will almost certainly be cheaper, so the first question would be to consider the viability of achieving a reliable sample using a self-completion questionnaire. If the questionnaire can be personally handed to customers and collected back from them, a reliable response rate will be easily achievable. Passengers on an aeroplane or customers in a restaurant would be good examples. Sometimes, as with shoppers in a store, personal collection and distribution is feasible but a suitable location for filling in the questionnaire would have to be provided.

For most organisations customers are more remote, so mail remains the only practical distribution option for a self-completion questionnaire. The probability of achieving an acceptable response rate will therefore have to be estimated. The key factor here is whether customers will perceive your organisation as an important supplier or your product as one in which they are very interested. If they do, it will be feasible to achieve a good response rate. If they do not, even following all the advice in this chapter will probably not be sufficient to lift the response rate to a reliable level. Examples of organisations in this position include utilities and many public services. In these cases, a telephone survey is the only sensible option.

Even when an adequate response rate can be achieved by mail, the telephone response rate will be higher and much more qualitative information will be gathered. In particular, reasons for low satisfaction can be probed and this will be very helpful when determining action plans after the survey. Telephone surveys are often the preferred option of many organisations both in business and consumer markets. A very large sample size is typically the main reason for selecting the postal option, since large samples will significantly increase the cost differential between postal and telephone surveys. A bank, for example, may want a reliable sample for each of several hundred branches and this would be extremely costly if customers were interviewed by telephone. Some sampling reliability may therefore have to be sacrificed in order to bring the project within budget.

5.7.2 Mixed methods

Sometimes it will be appropriate to mix the methods of data collection used in the same survey. This may happen quite often in business markets due to the very large differences in the value of large and small accounts. Just as the organisation invests more in servicing its key accounts, it might also choose to invest more in surveying them. Personal interviews might therefore be used for key accounts since a longer interview will be possible and this will enable the organisation to gain a greater depth of understanding of key accounts' perceptions. It will also have relationship benefits since it will demonstrate to the key accounts that they are considered to be very important, an impression that may not be conveyed by a telephone interview or a postal survey. The data collection methods could be mixed even further with telephone interviews used for medium value accounts and a postal survey for small ones.

Provided the same questions are asked in the same way, the responses will be comparable but it is important to ensure that this happens. Any additional discussion or additional questions used in the personal interviews with key accounts must come after the core questions from the telephone and postal surveys to ensure that additional discussions (which are absent from the telephone and postal surveys) cannot influence the respondents' answers to the core questions. Although the responses to the questions will be comparable, the reliability of the results across the three methods may not be. It is likely that lower response rates will reduce the reliability of the results from the low value customers compared with the other two segments, but this may be considered by many organisations to be a price worth paying. Assuming that the alternative would be a telephone survey across the board, the net effect of this three-tiered approach is to shift investment in the survey from the low value accounts to the key accounts, a decision that is likely to be compatible with the organisation's normal approach to resource allocation across the segments.

5.8 Confidentiality

There has been much debate about whether respondents should be anonymous or named in customer satisfaction surveys. Before suggesting an approach, we will review both sides of the confidentiality debate.

5.8.1 Confidentiality – the advantages

In the market research industry, respondent anonymity has traditionally been the norm on the assumption that confidentiality is more likely to elicit an impartial response from interviewees. This is based on evidence showing that respondents' answers can differ significantly when they are interviewed by people whom they know. If you are likely to have a continuing relationship with someone in the future, you may not want to offend them and you may want to protect a future negotiating stance. For example, if a salesman personally conducts a customer satisfaction interview with his customers, are they likely to give honest answers to questions about the performance of the salesman or about their satisfaction with current price levels? Even if the salesman does not personally conduct the interview (or if a self-completion questionnaire is used), the respondent's answers may still be influenced if he knows that they will be attributed to him and the salesman will see them.

Confidentiality is also supported if you think about the distinctive role of customer research compared with other customer management initiatives. Research should focus on the 'big picture' rather than on individual customers. It is normally undertaken with a sample of customers rather than a census but is intended to accurately represent the entire customer base. Its value for management decision making is in highlighting trends, problems with processes, widely held customer irritations which can be addressed by introducing improvements that benefit all customers and improve the company's position in the marketplace. The purpose of research is not to highlight specific problems with individual customers for two reasons. First, even a very serious problem (between one customer and an individual sales person, for example), may not be representative of a wider problem that needs corrective action. Second, research is not the best way to identify specific problems with individual customers. Organisations should have effective CRM programmes and complaints systems for this purpose. Relying on a periodic survey of a sample of customers to identify problems with individual customers suggests very poor customer management.

Whatever the frequency of customer satisfaction surveys, when they take place repeatedly customers learn about the process and draw conclusions that affect their future behaviour. If they can be open and honest without any personal repercussions, they are more likely to be honest in future surveys. On the other hand, if they learn that the organisation, their sales person or any other employee is using their survey response to manage their specific relationship with that supplier, they may gradually learn to 'use' the survey process. At first they may simply avoid making negative comments that may harm personal relationships with one or more employees of the supplier but over time they may learn to become more manipulative, seeking to use the survey process to influence pricing, service levels or other aspects of the cost benefit equation.

5.8.2 Confidentiality – the disadvantages

The obvious disadvantage of respondent confidentiality is that it gives the organisation no opportunity to respond to and fix any serious problems causing dissatisfaction and perhaps imminent defection of individual customers. Some organisations see the customer satisfaction survey as an additional service recovery opportunity, using a 'hot alert system' to immediately highlight any serious problems with individual customers, so that they can be resolved. Companies using this approach maintain that the opportunity to prevent possible customer defections outweighs the advantages of respondent confidentiality. Even one potential defection is worth averting.

In business markets, particularly those with very close customer–supplier relationships, the case against confidentiality may be even stronger. In these circumstances, suppliers may feel that customers would expect them to know what they had said in the survey and to respond with proposals to address their specific problems.

A further advantage of naming respondents is that their responses can be added to the customer database and modelling techniques can be used to project responses onto other, similar customer types. For organisations with a very large customer base this can be very helpful in classifying customers and identifying segments of customers for tailored CRM initiatives.

5.8.3 The right approach to respondent confidentiality

Our view is that the most important principle underpinning any survey is that the views collected should accurately represent the views held by respondents. If there is a chance that withholding respondent confidentiality could compromise the reliability of the data collected, the price paid for knowing 'who said what' is far too high. Faced with a forced trade-off, we would opt for respondent confidentiality every time. However, a compromise approach is possible. Respondents can be promised confidentiality but at the end of the interview, with full knowledge of what they were asked and how they replied, can be asked whether they wish to remain anonymous or whether they would prefer to have their comments (not their scores) linked with their name. Some customers, especially those in business markets who have developed a partnership approach with suppliers, will prefer their comments to be attributed to them. Equally, for those who prefer anonymity, the confidentiality of the interview and the survey process will be protected. With this approach, a hot alert system can still be used, but only with respondents who have consented to being named. Of course, if an organisation decides that its survey will not be anonymous this must be made totally clear to respondents before they take part.

5.9 When to survey

The remaining decisions to be taken about the survey concern timing and frequency. Of these, frequency should be considered first.

5.9.1 Continuous tracking or baseline survey

Customer satisfaction surveys can be periodic or continuous. Surveys are more likely to be continuous when the customer–supplier relationship revolves around a specific event or transaction, such as taking out a mortgage, buying a computer, calling a helpline or going on vacation. In these circumstances it is very important that customers are surveyed very soon after the event before their memory fades. Surveying customers weeks after an uneventful stay in a hotel or a brief conversation with a telephone help desk are completely wasteful, but they often happen. Unless the event was very important, e.g. the purchase of a new car or a piece of capital equipment, customers should be surveyed no longer than one week after the event. Results from continuous tracking surveys are usually rolled up and reported periodically as sample size permits. Where customers are happy to be named, comments should be continuously monitored and an efficient hot alert system developed.

Event-driven surveys tend to be tactical in nature and operational in focus. They often feed quickly into action, are less likely to be confidential and more likely to be volatile. The closer to the event, the more volatile they will be. If customers are surveyed as they check out of a hotel, their responses will be very heavily influenced by their recent experience. A disappointing breakfast a few minutes earlier may result in poor satisfaction ratings across the board. So this type of 'post-transaction' survey may not give an accurate measure of customers' underlying satisfaction or be a reliable guide to future purchasing behaviour. The irate customer who was made to wait too long to check out of the hotel may vow, in the heat of the moment, not to return, but some weeks later when next booking a hotel, the incident will have waned in importance and a more measured purchase decision will be made. For this reason, a periodic 'baseline' survey of customers away from the point of sale and the time of purchase will usually provide a much more accurate measure of underlying customer satisfaction.

A baseline survey will be periodic and is more suited to ongoing customer–supplier relationships and is more strategic in focus. Questions will cover the total product and will focus on customers' most important requirements. Baseline surveys are normally conducted annually, but can be more frequent. Before making a decision on frequency it is useful to consider the issues highlighted by the Satisfaction Improvement Loop.

ISO 9001:2000 links customer focus and continuous improvement. As far as measuring customer satisfaction is concerned, the purpose is not to conduct a survey but to continually improve the company's ability to satisfy and retain its customers. The 'plan, measure, act, review' philosophy enshrined in ISO 9001:2000 should be applied to the frequency of surveys. There is no point measuring more frequently than you can act and review. Figure 5.4 illustrates the sequence of events that must occur before your next customer survey can be expected to show whether you have succeeded in improving customer satisfaction. If you survey with greater frequency than that sequence of events, how will the results of that survey contribute to your management decisions and actions? The question to consider is how long the Satisfaction Improvement Loop will take to unfold in your organisation. Unless you are very slow at making decisions or taking action it should not take more than one year but quarterly or six-monthly surveys will be appropriate only in rapidly changing markets and for fast-acting organisations.

Figure 5.4 The Satisfaction Improvement Loop

5.9.2 Timing

The main point about timing, especially for annual surveys is that it should be consistent. Don't survey in the summer one year and in the winter the following year. Any number of factors affecting the customer–supplier relationship could change across the seasons. You will be aware of significant seasonal events in your industry and these potentially distorting factors should be avoided as should annual price increases and their aftermath.

5.10 Conclusions

(a) ISO 9001:2000 requires organisations to monitor *'customer perception as to whether the organisation has met customer requirements.'* When customers are making supplier selection decisions, perception is reality, even if the customer's perception is not accurate.

(b) Apart from organisations with a very small customer base, an objective quantitative survey will be the only way to reliably measure customers' perceptions.

(c) To conduct a quantitative survey, most organisations will choose between a telephone survey and self-completion questionnaires, typically in the form of a postal survey. Of the two methods, postal surveys are cheapest but telephone surveys will usually provide more detail and greater reliability due to higher response rates.

(d) New technology will often be inappropriate for customer satisfaction measurement due to unrepresentative samples.

(e) Although it is normal to use one data collection method for the whole survey, approaches can be mixed provided core questions occur at the beginning of the questionnaire and are asked consistently across all methods used.

(f) To guarantee honest and objective answers, respondent confidentiality must be offered. If respondents are happy to be named, a hot alert system will enable the organisation to address any instances of high dissatisfaction.

(g) Annual baseline surveys will usually be most appropriate for organisations with ongoing customer relationships. For transaction specific relationships, a rolling event-driven survey should be administered at the conclusion of the process.

6

Questionnaire design

Summary

Having decided what type of survey to conduct, you are now in a position to design a suitable questionnaire. Good questionnaire design will be affected by many factors and this chapter will highlight:

(a) What we can deduce from the Standard about questionnaire design.
(b) How to ensure that your questionnaire is the right length.
(c) What sections should be included in your questionnaire and in what order.
(d) How to avoid common mistakes in questionnaire wording.
(e) Which is the most suitable rating scale for customer satisfaction measurement.

6.1 What the Standard says

The standard has nothing specific to say on the technicalities of questionnaire design. The only clues on questionnaire design are to be found in the 'monitoring and measurement' section, where clause 8.2.1, 'customer satisfaction', states:

As one of the measurements of the performance of the quality management system, the organisation shall monitor information relating to customer perception as to whether the organisation has met customer requirements. The methods for obtaining and using this information shall be determined.

There are two key indicators in this brief statement from the Standard. The first is that the organisation must measure whether it has met customers' requirements and this, in turn, has two implications for questionnaire design. The first implication was covered in Chapter 3, where we established that in order to measure whether customers' requirements are being met, the questions asked must focus on customers' main requirements. These will be established through exploratory research using the 'lens of the customer'. If the 'lens of the organisation' is used, and management asks questions on the topics they wish to cover, the survey will not provide a measure of whether customers' requirements have been met. The second implication is that the questionnaire must cover both sides of the equation that we established in our definition of customer satisfaction – importance and satisfaction, otherwise the relative importance of customers' requirements would never be reliably understood.

The second indicator in clause 8.2.1 is the phrase *'customer perception'*. The information collected and monitored will not necessarily be an accurate reflection of the organisation's real performance. It will be customers' perception of that performance. Customers' perceptions are not always fair or accurate, but they are the information on which customers base their judgements and future choice of supplier. It is therefore an accurate understanding of customers' perceptions that is the most useful measure for the organisation to monitor. This means that an objective customer survey is the only reliable way to collect this information and that the questionnaire should focus on eliciting customers' opinions and should definitely not attempt to lead customers, by providing information about the organisation's actual performance for example.

6.2 Questionnaire layout

Sample questionnaires covering all the aspects of questionnaire design explained in this chapter are shown in the appendices at the end of the book. The first thing to plan is the overall layout and the key issues here are summarised in Figure 6.1.

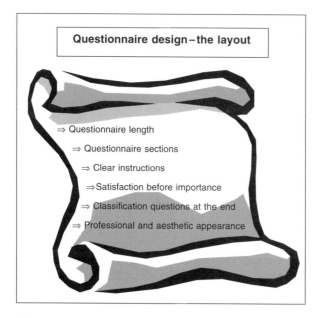

Figure 6.1 Questionnaire layout

6.2.1 Questionnaire length

Whether you are designing a self-completion questionnaire or one that will be administered by interview, 50 questions is a good guideline for maximum length. This will take around ten to fifteen minutes to complete whichever survey type is used. There will be some differences in wording and these will be explored later. With paper questionnaires you will find that 50 questions can be squeezed onto a double-sided questionnaire or can be spaced out to cover four sides. Tests show that although shorter questionnaires are desirable *per se*, the four-sided questionnaire is likely to achieve a higher response rate and a better quality of response because it will look more attractive and will be easier to navigate, understand and fill in. Some respondents may never start questionnaires that have small type or look cluttered as they will be seen as difficult to complete.

6.2.2 Questionnaire sections

The next stage is to divide the 50 questions into sections. The starting point is the list of the most important customer requirements identified in the exploratory research and they will have to be rated for importance as well as satisfaction. Precisely how many questions you include from the exploratory research will depend on how many additional questions you wish to ask. Most additional questions will be used to classify respondents, but there may be a few additional questions you wish to ask that have nothing to do with customer satisfaction. If you include the top 20 customer requirements from the exploratory research you will have used up 40 questions since each will have to be rated for importance as well as satisfaction. If you probe low satisfaction scores and ask for a comment explaining each one, this will generate an average of three additional questions per respondent. You are likely to have four or five questions to classify respondents, leaving a maximum of two or three questions for exploring other topics. You should resist the temptation to cut down on the number of customer requirements monitored in order to ask a larger number of additional questions. This is a customer satisfaction survey and that is where the focus should remain. If you try to pursue too many different objectives through one survey you will most likely achieve none properly. The questionnaire sections, together with a guide to the maximum number of questions allocated to each section, can be seen in Figure 6.2. Further explanation for some sections is provided below.

6.2.3 Instructions

The first thing respondents will see on the questionnaire will be the instructions and they have to be totally clear. If a questionnaire can be filled in wrongly you can be sure that some respondents will do it. So you have to have very clear instructions, even if that means that they take up quite a lot of space. You can find example of instructions in the sample questionnaires in the appendices at the end of the book.

Questionnaire sections	
Section	Maximum questions
Introduction	
Satisfaction scores	20
Probing low satisfaction scores	3
Importance scores	20
Additional questions	3
Classification questions	4

Figure 6.2 Questionnaire sections

6.2.4 Satisfaction and importance questions

The customer requirements must be covered in two separate sections for satisfaction and importance. It is tempting, but incorrect to cover both importance and satisfaction for each requirement before moving onto the next. If you adopt this approach you will get an unrealistic correlation between importance and satisfaction scores for each requirement. Separate importance and satisfaction sections should therefore be used, but in what order? Although it is conventional to ask the importance section before satisfaction, our tests at The Leadership Factor show that it is better to start with satisfaction scores since this makes respondents familiar with all the issues before they are asked to score importance. When the importance section follows satisfaction a wider range of importance scores is usually achieved and this provides greater discriminatory power at the analysis stage. Scores given for satisfaction vary little whether they are asked before or after importance.

So you should list the requirements and first rate them all for satisfaction. You should then probe all low satisfaction scores (effective only with interviews, not self-completion questionnaires) before listing all the requirements again and rating them for importance. But in what order should the requirements be listed? Strictly speaking they should be listed in a random order and, strictly speaking, not in the same order on every questionnaire, on the grounds the earlier questions might influence respondents' thinking on the later ones. Therefore, for really accurate research, the list of attributes should be rotated.

However, it would not be common practice to print ten different versions of a customer survey questionnaire so that the questions can be rotated. In reality, most commercial research would just print one version with the questions in the same order on every questionnaire. In deciding which order the questions should be in, there are two basic choices. One option is to base it on the sequence of events that customers typically go through when dealing with your company and that works very well for one-off events like taking out a mortgage or making an insurance claim. However, for many organisations that have ongoing relationships with customers involving a variety of contacts for different things at different times, using the sequence of events as a basis for question order will not work. In that situation it would be normal to use topic groupings, with all the questions on quality grouped together, all the questions on delivery together etc.

6.2.5 Classification questions

Classification questions should come at the end. Some people may be offended by what they see as impertinent questions about age, occupation or income, so it is always better to leave classification questions until after they have answered the other questions. The one exception here would be quota samples where respondents have to be qualified before their inclusion in the survey.

6.2.6 Design issues

This advice applies only to self-completion questionnaires, which need to look professional and aesthetically appealing. We have already suggested that questions should be spaced out, with an attractive layout even if it makes the questionnaire run into more pages. Use of colour is also worthwhile. Even a two-colour questionnaire can appear much more attractive because semi-tones can be used very effectively for clarification and differentiation.

6.3 Questionnaire wording

Figure 6.3 shows a checklist. You could compare your questionnaire with this checklist and ask whether it breaks any of the wording rules listed.

6.3.1 Knowledgeable answers

The first thing to consider is whether respondents will possess the knowledge to answer the questions you have asked. Not having it won't stop them! People tend to think that they ought to have an opinion on things. You might be asking passengers at an airport for their views on the differences between economy and business class flights. Many people would answer those questions even if they have never flown business class. That would not be a problem if you want to understand economy class passengers' perceptions of business class travel, but it would be very misleading if you were trying to understand the real experiences of business class customers. So, if you only wanted people who had flown business class, you would have to qualify respondents before including them in the survey.

A related problem is that respondents may not have experience of your organisation's performance on all the requirements covered. The Chief

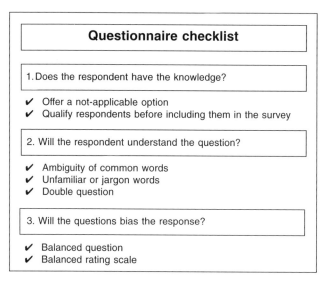

Figure 6.3 Questionnaire wording

Executive, for example, may not have any real knowledge of your on-time-delivery performance. To avoid gathering misleading scores from ill informed members of the DMU, you should clearly offer a 'not applicable' option for each satisfaction question. It is not necessary to provide a 'not applicable' option for importance scores since respondents will have a view on the relative importance of each requirement including those with which they are not personally involved.

6.3.2 No ambiguous questions

The second thing to consider is whether the respondents will understand the questions, or, more accurately, whether they will all assign to the questions the same meaning as the author of the questionnaire. There are several potential problems here, often because many of the words we use quite happily in everyday speech are dangerous when used in questionnaires because they are just not precise enough. A pertinent example is shown in Figure 6.4.

What exactly does the word 'regularly' mean exactly? When the results of that question have been analysed, what will they tell anybody? 'Regularly' could mean anything from every day to annually. When wording questions you have to be extremely precise, to the point of being pedantic. You cannot afford any ambiguity or you may find that you have generated a meaningless set of results on completion of your survey. So the question about the newspapers would have to be phrased as in Figure 6.5.

6.3.3 No jargon

Another reason why respondents misunderstand questions is the use of unfamiliar

Which of the following newspapers do you read regularly?

Please tick the box next to any newspapers that you read regularly:

Express ☐	Mirror ☐
Guardian ☐	Sun ☐
Mail ☐	Times ☐

Figure 6.4 Ambiguous question

How often do you read each of the following newspapers?
Please tick one box for each newspaper

	Every day	More than once a week	Weekly	Monthly	Every 3 months	Less than once every 3 months	Never
Express	☐	☐	☐	☐	☐	☐	☐
Guardian	☐	☐	☐	☐	☐	☐	☐
Mail	☐	☐	☐	☐	☐	☐	☐
Mirror	☐	☐	☐	☐	☐	☐	☐
Sun	☐	☐	☐	☐	☐	☐	☐
Times	☐	☐	☐	☐	☐	☐	☐

Figure 6.5 Precise question

words. Everybody knows it is not advisable to use jargon but most people still underestimate the extent to which words they use all the time at work with colleagues can be jargon words to customers. Of course, that is another very good reason for carrying out the exploratory research because you can use the customers' terminology on the questionnaire rather than your own. As well as obviously technical names, even words such as facility and amenity are liable to ambiguity and misinterpretation.

6.3.4 No double questions

Double questions are a very common reason for misunderstanding and result in unactionable survey results. A common example from customer surveys would be:

Were the staff friendly and helpful?

Which characteristic do you want to know about? Friendliness and helpfulness are not the same are they? If that question is scored poorly, indicating customer dissatisfaction, how would the organisation know what to change to put matters right? If you want to include both those aspects of staff behaviour in the questionnaire, you have to ask two questions.

6.3.5 No biased questions

Probably the biggest problem on the wording of questionnaires is the danger that the questionnaire itself will bias the response. There are two reasons why this might happen. Firstly the question itself and secondly the rating scale. Typical questions on a customer satisfaction survey might be:

How satisfied are you with the variety of food on the menu?
How satisfied are you with the speed of response for on-site technical support?
How satisfied are you with the reliability of the product?

Each one of those questions has introduced an element of bias which is likely to skew the results, and the problem arises in the first part of the question:

How satisfied are you with . . . ?

The question itself is suggesting that customers are satisfied. It is just a matter of how satisfied. To eliminate that bias and be certain that the survey is providing an accurate measure of customer satisfaction, those questions should be worded as follows:

How satisfied or dissatisfied are you with the variety of food on the menu?
How satisfied or dissatisfied are you with the speed of response for on-site technical support?
How satisfied or dissatisfied are you with the reliability of the product?

6.3.6 No biased rating scales

The other part of the question that might bias the response is the rating scale. Biased rating scales are commonly found on many customer satisfaction questionnaires, as shown in Figure 6.6.

The scale shown in Figure 6.6 is not balanced and is likely to bias the result towards satisfaction. Most positively biased rating scales on customer satisfaction questionnaires are probably there because the questionnaire

Please comment on our quality of service by ticking one box on each line:

	Excellent	Good	Average	Poor
Helpfulness of staff	☐	☐	☐	☐
Friendliness of staff	☐	☐	☐	☐
Cleanliness of the restaurant	☐	☐	☐	☐
Cleanliness of the toilets	☐	☐	☐	☐
Waiting time for your table	☐	☐	☐	☐
Waiting time for your meal	☐	☐	☐	☐

Figure 6.6 A positively biased rating scale

designers are oblivious of the problem. However, some companies who are very experienced in CSM deliberately use positively biased questionnaires on the grounds that only 'top box' satisfaction matters, so it is only degrees of satisfaction that are worth measuring. We feel that there are two problems with this philosophy. Firstly, even if most customers are somewhere in the very satisfied zone, it is still essential information to understand just how dissatisfied the least satisfied customers are and the extent to which individual attributes are causing the problem. In many ways it is more valuable to the organisation to identify in detail the problem areas that it can fix than to have detailed information on how satisfied its most satisfied customers are. The second argument against using positively biased rating scales is that it just is not necessary. If you have a sufficient number of points on the scale you can accommodate degrees of satisfaction and dissatisfaction in equal proportions, as shown in Figure 6.7.

How satisfied or dissatisfied are you with the reliability of our delivery times?

Tick one box

Totally satisfied	☐
Very satisfied	☐
Quite satisfied	☐
Neither satisfied nor dissatisfied	☐
Quite dissatisfied	☐
Very dissatisfied	☐
Totally dissatisfied	☐

Figure 6.7 A balanced rating scale

Figure 6.7 is a balanced rating scale because it has an equal number of points above and below the mid-point and, very importantly, the words at opposing points on the scale are exact opposites of each other. Whether or not it has a mid-point makes no difference to whether or not it is balanced. There is much interest in whether scales should have a mid-point. Strictly speaking, a scale should have a mid-point on the grounds that it is not valid research to force anyone to express an opinion they don't hold. For example an interviewer may approach people in the street and ask them:

Who are you going to vote for at the next election?

Some people will reply

I don't know.

If the interviewer then pressurises respondents to provide a definitive answer, so that eventually, to bring the interview to a close, the respondent nominates one of the political parties, that would not be acceptable research. 'Don't know' is a valid response.

So strictly speaking you should have a middle option but you do not need to worry about everybody ticking it. It is a myth that everybody makes a beeline for the middle option as though it is an easy option and saves them from having to think. They do tend to put what they think and you do get a range of answers. What is true is that respondents sometimes avoid the extremes of the scale. So if it does look as though the scores are clustered around the middle it is probably not because respondents are aiming for the middle but because they are avoiding the extremes. Of course, that can be a problem if you have only used a five-point scale because if some respondents avoid the extremes they only have three points left to choose between. However, there are many things to consider when selecting the most appropriate type of rating scale and these issues are now examined in the next section.

6.4 Rating scales

The third key aspect of questionnaire design is the rating scale and since CSM is about measuring satisfaction and the rating scale is the tool used to do the measuring, it is a very critical element. The three most commonly used scales in customer satisfaction research are Likert scales, verbal scales and numerical scales. The Likert and verbal scales are similar in that they both use words to describe the points on the scale. The numerical scale, as expected, uses numbers. Figures 6.8 to 6.10 show examples of each scale.

6.4.1 Likert scale

Very common in many types of attitude research, the Likert scale is easy to fill in but does have the considerable disadvantage that the bold statement

Likert scale

Satisfaction

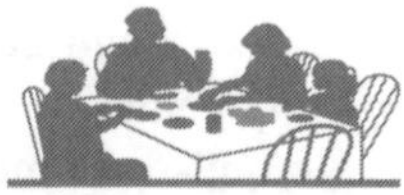

Below are some features of eating out at_______. Please place an 'X' in the box which most accurately reflects how much you agree or disagree with the statement or in the N/A box if it is not relevant to you

	N/A	Disagree strongly	Disagree slightly	Neither agree nor disagree	Agree slightly	Agree strongly
1. The restaurant was clean	☐	☐	☐	☐	☐	☐
2. The service was quick	☐	☐	☐	☐	☐	☐
3. The food was high quality	☐	☐	☐	☐	☐	☐

Importance

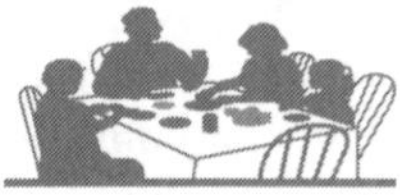

Please read the following statements and place an 'X' in the box that most accurately reflects how much you agree or disagree with the statement

	Disagree strongly	Disagree slightly	Neither agree nor disagree	Agree slightly	Agree strongly
1. When eating out it is important that the restaurant is clean	☐	☐	☐	☐	☐
2. When eating out quick service is important	☐	☐	☐	☐	☐
3. When eating out it is important that the food is high quality	☐	☐	☐	☐	☐

Figure 6.8 Likert scale

may bias respondents' answers. Likert scales on satisfaction questionnaires are always positively biased. You very rarely see negatively biased ones using examples of appalling service for the bold statements. ('*The restaurant was filthy . . . agree – disagree*'). Bias is even more likely on importance questions where the respondent is effectively being told '*it is important that . . .*'

6.4.2 Verbal scale

Questionnaires using verbal scales are easy to complete and have the advantage of incorporating the concepts being measured (importance and satisfaction) into the scale, thus reducing the risk of respondent confusion. Since the verbal scale is the simplest and clearest it is likely to be the one most accurately completed with the fewest errors. Reporting verbal scales on the basis of 'percentage satisfied' (i.e. those ticking the top two boxes) can mask changes

Verbal scale

Satisfaction

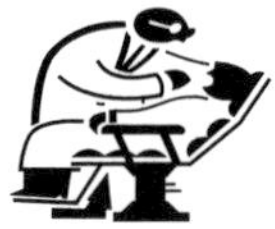

Below are some features of visiting______Dental Practice. Please place an 'X' in the box which most accurately reflects how *satisfied* or *dissatisfied* you are with each item or put an 'X' in the N/A box if it is not relevant to you

	N/A	Very dis-satisfied	Quite dis-satisfied	Neither satisfied nor dis-satisfied	Quite satisfied	Very satisfied
1. Helpfulness of reception staff	☐	☐	☐	☐	☐	☐
2. Location of the surgery	☐	☐	☐	☐	☐	☐
3. Cost of the dental treatment	☐	☐	☐	☐	☐	☐

Importance

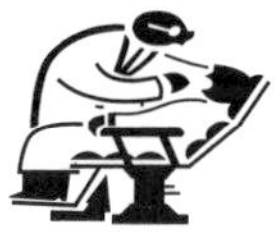

Below are some features of visiting the dentist. Please place an 'X' in the box that most accurately reflects how *important* or *unimportant* each feature is to you

	Very un-important	Quite un-important	Neither important nor un-important	Quite important	Very important
1. Helpfulness of reception staff	☐	☐	☐	☐	☐
2. Location of the surgery	☐	☐	☐	☐	☐
3. Cost of the dental treatment	☐	☐	☐	☐	☐

Figure 6.9 Verbal scale

in customer satisfaction caused by the mix of scores in the 'satisfied' and 'dissatisfied' categories. In fact, if results are reported in this way there is no reason to have more than two points on the scale – satisfied and dissatisfied.

It is not statistically acceptable to convert the points on a verbal scale into numbers and generate a mean score from those numbers. This is because verbal type scales are ordinal in function. They give an order from good to bad or satisfied to dissatisfied without quantifying it. In other words, we know that 'strongly agree' is better than 'agree' but we don't know by how much. Nor do we know if the distance between 'strongly agree' and 'agree' is the same as the distance between 'agree' and 'neither agree nor disagree'. Therefore, verbal scales have to be analysed using a frequency distribution, which simply involves counting how many respondents ticked each box. It is not statistically acceptable to use means and standard deviations or to apply most multivariate statistical techniques to establish the relationships between variables in the data set. This makes it impossible to make a direct comparison

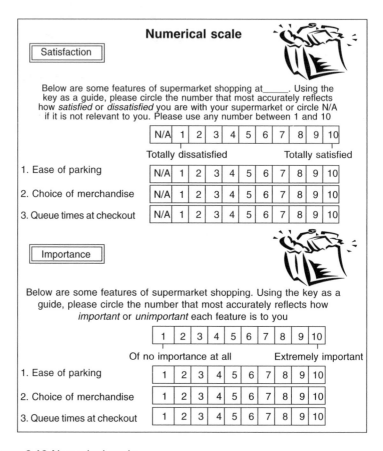

Figure 6.10 Numerical scale

of importance and satisfaction unless points on the scale are grouped, e.g. percentage of respondents ticking 'very satisfied' and 'satisfied' versus percentage ticking 'very important' and 'important'. As indicated previously due to potential large variations in the distribution of scores within these broad categories, such results may not paint a reliable picture.

6.4.3 Numerical scale

Numerical scales are easy to fill in – virtually as easy as verbal scales. Unlike most other scales, the numerical scale can be used whatever the method of data collection. Verbal scales are very clumsy if telephone interviews are used.

A very strong argument in favour of the numerical scale is its user friendliness when it comes to analysing and, very importantly, communicating the results to colleagues in your organisation. The simple average scores generated by the 10-point numerical scale are easy for everyone to understand and paint a very clear picture of the results and their implications. When compared directly with average scores for importance, they clearly illustrate the areas to address, compared with the far less graphic frequency distributions which must be used for statistically valid analysis of verbal type scales. This is an extremely important factor in favour of using numerical scales for CSM questionnaires because internal feedback is where the CSM process fails in many organisations. There is simply insufficient company-wide understanding of the areas where service improvement efforts should be focused. Having clear and simple results from the survey, which all staff can immediately understand, is the essential starting point in this battle for hearts and minds.

Numerical scales also make it possible to have a wider scale. They most commonly have 5, 7 or 10 points. It is not practical to have many points on a verbal type scale and this is a considerable disadvantage since the differences between satisfaction survey results from one period to the next will often be very small. A wider scale enables the respondent to be more discriminating especially at the satisfied end of the scale, which is important since it is only the very satisfied who are likely to recommend and to remain loyal if services become competitive.

More points also yield greater variability, which is better for analytical purposes for two main reasons. First, scales with more points discriminate better between top and poor performers so tend to have greater utility for management decision making and tracking. Second, it is easier to establish 'covariance' between two variables with greater dispersion (i.e. variance around their means). Covariance is critical to the development of robust models such as those identifying the drivers of customer satisfaction (see Chapter 7).

Sample questionnaires using a 10-point numerical scale are provided at the end of the book. Appendix B shows an example of a self-completion questionnaire and Appendix A an example of a questionnaire for a telephone interview.

6.5 Conclusions

(a) ISO 9001:2000 specifies that the organisation must measure '*customer perception as to whether the organisation has met customer requirements.*' This means that the questions must be based on customers' main requirements, as identified by exploratory research and that the organisation must monitor customers' opinions about its performance. Whilst these perceptions may not always accord with reality, they do form the basis on which customers make supplier selection decisions.

(b) Questionnaires should contain no more than 50 questions and, if self-completion, should be spread across four sides of paper rather than compressed onto two.

(c) Satisfaction and importance should be scored in separate sections with satisfaction asked first.

(d) Low satisfaction scores should be probed to understand the reasons in more depth.

(e) Classification questions should always come at the end of the questionnaire.
(f) To maximise the reliability of customers' answers, they should be offered a not-applicable option for issues where their experience and knowledge is sparse. Where necessary, qualify respondents' suitability for inclusion in the survey before beginning an interview.
(g) To avoid ambiguity and misinterpretation, questionnaire wording has to be very precise and jargon-free.
(h) Double questions must be avoided.
(i) Researchers must be conscious of the risk of introducing bias to the survey by asking unbalanced questions or by using an unbalanced rating scale.
(j) Numerical rating scales are most suitable for customer satisfaction measurement because they offer greater analytical potential and they make it easier to get the message across to employees after the survey.
(k) Scales with more points are better than those with fewer because they have greater discriminatory powers and movements in customer satisfaction are usually small. A 10-point numerical rating scale is recommended.

7

Analysis of data

Summary

Whether the survey involves interviews or self-completion methods, a large, sometimes very large, volume of questionnaires will be generated. This data needs to be analysed and reported. In this chapter we will cover the techniques typically used to analyse CSM surveys. Charts to illustrate the outcomes will accompany the explanations in this chapter. Any data included in the charts and tables is fictitious and does not apply to any specific organisation. The key points to be covered include:

(a) Computer and software issues.
(b) How to analyse numerical scales.
(c) How to analyse verbal scales.
(d) Identifying priorities for improvement.
(e) Calculating a headline Customer Satisfaction Index.

7.1 What the Standard says

'Measurement, analysis and improvement' is covered in Section 8 of ISO 9001:2000. The first clause makes the following general comments:

8.1 General
The organisation shall plan and implement the monitoring, measurement, analysis and improvement processes needed

(a) To demonstrate conformity of the product
(b) To ensure conformity of the quality management system, and
(c) To continually improve the effectiveness of the quality management system.

This shall include determination of applicable methods, including statistical techniques, and the extent of their use.

This suggests that the statistical techniques used for analysis of CSM data (see clause 8.4 of the Standard) could be determined by the organisation.

However, for most organisations with a customer base of reasonable size, an objective quantitative survey is going to be the 'applicable method'. For organisations with a very small number of customers a more qualitative approach may be justifiable in ISO terms, but this will be a very small percentage of ISO 9001 registered organisations. Clause 8.4 provides more detail on the analysis of information.

> *8.4 Analysis of data*
> *The organisation shall determine, collect and analyse appropriate data to demonstrate the suitability and effectiveness of the quality management system and to evaluate where continual improvement of the effectiveness of the quality management system can be made. This shall include data generated as a result of monitoring and measurement and from other relevant sources.*
> *The analysis of data shall provide information relating to*
>
> *(a) Customer satisfaction (see 8.2.1)*
> *(b) Conformity to product requirements (see 7.2.1).*

Since the standard also stipulates the use of recognised analytical and statistical techniques, and the Introduction (Para 02 Process approach) refers to '*continual improvement of processes based on **objective measurement***', it will be necessary to formally survey customers rather than informally consult them during the normal course of business.

7.2 Manual or computerised analysis

Computers have three main advantages over manual analysis:

(i)   they can handle large volumes of data quickly and easily, performing a range of statistical analyses almost instantly;
(ii)   raw data and your analyses can be stored and easily revisited at a later date if further work is required;
(iii) a wide range of graphs and charts can be easily produced from the stored data.

As with many other tasks, the main disadvantage of using computers for analysing survey results lies in the expertise required to manipulate the software. Computer experts will almost invariably benefit from adopting computerised analysis, however small the survey, because of the advantages of high quality graphical presentation and subsequent data retrieval. If you are not computer literate, mastering any appropriate software will take time and you may feel that the time is not warranted if your survey involves relatively small numbers, e.g. below 100 respondents and your surveys, and therefore your use of the software, would be infrequent, e.g. annually or longer.

If you meet these two criteria and you are not already familiar with appropriate software your investment of time may outweigh the advantages of using the computer and with long intervals between usage you would probably have to repeat most of the learning curve on each occasion. In that situation manual analysis is quite feasible and if you use a scientific calculator you will be able to carry out all the statistical analyses recommended in this chapter. Cross-tabulations to analyse segment details are very time consuming manually, but with small samples, would probably not be necessary anyway. Another drawback of using a calculator is that data input errors are easy to make and impossible to trace. Therefore, the only way to ensure an error-free outcome is to key in each set of data twice, proceeding only if the totals are identical. When using a calculator it is often more efficient to work in pairs, one calling out the values and the other entering them. Having completed your manual analysis you will still need to display the results, which usually brings us back to computers again, although more user-friendly software, such as word processors, will often be adequate for this purpose. In conclusion, there are many arguments in favour of computer analysis, even for small surveys, so if your organisation possesses appropriate software and someone who can use it you would be well advised to take the computerised option. For the truly computer-phobic, data analysis services are provided by most market research companies. You simply provide your raw data and agree the statistical analyses that you require. You can also commission appropriate charts and graphs, presentation materials and even report writing.

7.3 Computer software

There is a wide choice of specialist software for analysing survey results. Two simple packages used by market researchers are '*SNAP*', developed by Mercator Computer Systems and '*Pinpoint*' by Longman Logotron. Both are designed to be user friendly to market researchers. Basically, the programs allow you to design your questionnaire on the screen and after the survey to enter results directly onto questionnaires on the screen. This makes data entry very easy and helps to minimise errors. The software can then carry out all the normal statistical analyses and display the result in table or chart form.

SPSS by SPSS (UK) Ltd is a much more sophisticated statistical analysis package with several modules covering advanced analytical techniques such as multivariate statistics, structural equation modelling, correspondence analysis, conjoint analysis and other techniques not necessary for basic analysis of customer satisfaction survey data.

An obvious alternative to the specialist software mentioned above is a basic spreadsheet package such as Microsoft Excel. The big advantage of using a standard spreadsheet package is that these will already be found within most organisations together with people who have the skills to use it. There are also reporting advantages since there will be a wide range of graphical options for displaying results which can be linked into sister packages for word processing reports or producing slides for presentations. Compared with the specialist research packages, the only disadvantage is that a spreadsheet database has to be compiled for each survey, with columns for each question, one row assigned to each respondent and appropriate analyses programmed in to the columns at the foot of the spreadsheet, as shown in Figure 7.1. However, for anyone with reasonable spreadsheet skills this is a very simple task.

7.4 Analysing the results

7.4.1 Analysing numerical scales

Having interviewed a large number of customers to measure their individual satisfaction levels, there are several statistical analyses that should be carried out if you are to draw accurate conclusions about the satisfaction of the customer base as a whole.

7.4.1.1 Average

More accurately defined as the arithmetic mean, the average of a string of values is the most commonly used measure to report the scores given for each requirement both for importance and satisfaction. It is easy to communicate and widely understood provided a suitable rating scale (e.g. a 10-point numerical scale) has been used. However, this common sense average can occasionally provide misleading results, so it is prudent to supplement the arithmetic mean with some additional analyses to confirm the validity of your conclusions.

7.4.1.2 Range

Whatever the rating scale it is useful to know the range of marks given as well as the average. An apparently satisfactory average score of 8.6 out of 10 could hide a wide range of individual scores possibly including a small minority of highly dissatisfied customers. The range is simply the difference between the highest and lowest scores in the column of values.

The range is not a very satisfactory measure since it is based on only two of the values in the entire list of numbers. This could be misleading if either the highest or the lowest values are extreme scores, as shown by the values for Question 3 in Figure 7.1, where the range is 9. Comparing the scores for Question 3 with those for Question 5 shows the danger of relying on the range as a measure of dispersion. Both have the same average score, but the range of values for Question 3 is 9 and for Question 5 the range is 4, suggesting a much more diverse spread of opinion for Question 3. In reality, the views of most respondents on Question 3 are quite close. Without the one extreme

Analysis of data						
Respondent	Question 1	Question 2	Question 3	Question 4	Question 5	Question 6
1	9	7	8	10	9	10
2	9	7	10	10	6	10
3	8	8	8	4	8	10
4	10	7	9	9	10	9
5	10	10	1	5	–	6
6	8	7	8	8	7	10
7	9	7	9	10	9	6
8	9	9	8	9	6	7
9	8	7	9	4	8	9
10	10	7	8	9	7	7
Average	9	7.6	7.8	7.8	7.8	8.4
High	10	10	10	10	10	10
Low	8	7	1	4	6	6
Standard deviation	0.77	1.02	2.36	2.36	1.31	1.62
Median	9	7	8	9	8	9
Mode	9	7	8	9	6, 7, 8, 9	10
Base	10	10	10	10	9	10

Figure 7.1 Sample data

value for Question 3, the range would only be 3, which is lower than the range for Question 5.

7.4.1.3   Standard deviation

The standard deviation is less affected than the range by extreme values. It is a very accurate measure for showing how closely the values in a list cluster around or diverge from the average. The standard deviation is lower if the values cluster closely around the mean and becomes higher the more they diverge from it. For the mathematically inclined, the standard deviation is defined as the square root of the variance, with the formula shown in Figure 7.2.

Using the list of values in Question 3, the calculation of the standard deviation is shown in Figure 7.3.

Comparing the data for Questions 3 and 4 shows the limitation of the range indicator and the usefulness of the standard deviation. Although the range for Question 3 is 50% greater (9 compared with 6), the standard deviations

$$\sqrt{\frac{\Sigma\,(x - \bar{x})^2}{n}}$$

Figure 7.2 Standard deviation formula

Value		Variance is difference between value and average value	Variance squared
	(X)	(X–X̄)	(X–X̄)²
	8	0.2	0.04
	10	2.2	4.84
	8	0.2	0.04
	9	1.2	1.44
	1	−6.8	46.24
	8	0.2	0.04
	9	1.2	1.44
	8	0.2	0.04
	9	1.2	1.44
	8	0.2	0.04
Totals	78	0	55.60
Average	7.8		5.56
The standard deviation is the square root of 5.56, i.e. 2.36			

Figure 7.3 Calculating the standard deviation

for the two questions are the same. This is produced by the greater number of values (4s, 5s and 10s) that diverge from the mean in the Question 4 column. In fact, if Table 7.1 showed a more typical sample size (e.g. 100 respondents) a single extreme value such as the 1/10 in the Question 3 column would have far less impact on the standard deviation. However, if the bi-polar pattern shown in the Question 4 column (people either score very high or quite low, with very few respondents occupying the middle ground) were repeated over a much larger sample size, its standard deviation would remain similar. This is a very useful feature in customer satisfaction measurement for demonstrating that the average score may be a misleading measure because customers cluster into two or more groupings.

A high standard deviation may be seen for some importance scores. For example, buying at the lowest possible price may be very important to some customers but far less important to others. This variance in customers' priorities can be a very effective way of segmenting markets according to customer needs.

7.4.1.4 The median

The median is the true middle score – i.e. the middle of a list of numbers when all the values are arranged in order of magnitude. The median is sometimes preferred to the mean as a true average if a small number of very wayward values significantly distort the arithmetic mean. A good example would be overdue deliveries. A firm may have recorded ten late deliveries in the previous month as shown in Figure 7.4. Typically, overdue deliveries are one, two or at most, three days late, but the occasional delay with a bought-in component or a major design problem might exceptionally result in a seriously overdue delivery.

In this example the median lateness is clearly more representative of the real situation, although monitoring the maximum would also be useful. In customer satisfaction measurement, however, it is unusual for the median value to be a more useful indicator than the arithmetic mean. One reason for this is the relatively narrow range of the commonly used rating scales, making it impossible for exceptional values to diverge as excessively as the example shown in Figure 7.4. The second problem with the median for customer survey analysis is that it will typically be a round number, and with suppliers tracking very small shifts in average scores the median is unable to provide the required accuracy.

Overdue deliveries		
Delivery number	Despatch date	Days overdue
21 680	04/10/95	1
21 698	05/10/95	1
21 731	09/10/95	1
21 731	20/10/95	1
21 696	09/10/95	2
21 720	13/10/95	2
21 721	13/10/95	2
21 760	18/10/95	2
21 784	25/10/95	3
21 582	26/10/95	48
Mean lateness = 6.3 days Median lateness = 2 days		

Figure 7.4 Mean and median averages

7.4.1.5 Base

The final row in Figure 7.1 simply counts the number of cells in which a value exists. This will demonstrate if large numbers of respondents have been unable to answer a particular question, which may point to a problem area. For example, if a significant number of respondents felt unable to rate the supplier on its environmental management, and the company was registered to the ISO 14 000 standard, it would have identified a need to educate its customer base, however high the average score of those respondents who did express an opinion.

7.4.1.6 Cross-tabulations

One of the most interesting and revealing analyses to undertake is the cross-tabulation which extracts and compares subsets of data. This enables comparison between the views of different segments such as purchasing managers versus production managers or young people compared with older people. It enables the supplier to understand if different groups of customers have different needs and priorities, or to see if it is rated more highly in some market segments than in others. If so, it can consider why it is rated more highly in its stronger segments and use those conclusions for strategic decision making. Cross-tabulations can be used to examine any type of segment, provided respondents have been appropriately classified. There is a strong argument for including as many classification categories as possible at the survey design stage since the cross-tabulation function can be used only if the segment data has been recorded on the questionnaire.

7.4.2 Analysing verbal scales

If verbal type scales are used for questionnaires, the results have to be analysed using a frequency distribution – in other words, how many people said what. A frequency distribution is shown in Figure 7.5. The numbers are usually

	Very satisfied	Quite satisfied	Neither satisfied nor dissatisfied	Quite dissatisfied	Very dissatisfied
Opening hours	34	27	6	21	12
Queueing time	4	18	48	19	11
Courtesy of staff	47	31	20	2	0
Knowledge of staff	16	26	28	23	7
Friendliness of staff	32	24	23	10	1
Appearance of staff	40	44	16	0	0

Figure 7.5 Frequency distribution

percentages, so in the example shown, 34% are very satisfied with the opening hours, 27% are quite satisfied. It is a totally accurate summary of the results, but it does not make a very strong impression compared with the kind of charts that can be produced with average scores (see Section 7.5).

It would be possible to produce charts for individual attributes, each with five bars showing varying levels of satisfaction or importance by attribute. However, the real problem is the absence of a single average score for each attribute. For example, it is not possible to make a direct comparison between the importance score for opening hours and the satisfaction score for opening hours, so you cannot carry out a gap analysis to arrive at the PFIs (see Section 7.5). That is a major disadvantage of using a verbal type scale because what you can do with the results is very limited compared with the numerical scale.

Some people look at the data they get from verbal type scales, recognise the limitations and realise that it would be much more useful to have average scores. They try to solve the problem by changing the points on the verbal scale into numbers and carry on as though they had used a numerical scale from the outset. People change five-point verbal type scales into various numerical scales as shown in Figure 7.6.

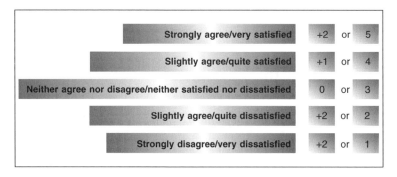

Figure 7.6 Changing verbal to numerical scales

The numerical data in Figure 7.6 illustrates one of the problems. Once you decide to change the information given to you by the customers, what do you change it into? The two sets of numbers shown in the table will not give the same result. Even if everybody standardised on the 5-4-3-2-1 scale, how can you be sure that a customer who responded 'quite satisfied' would have scored 4 on the numerical scale? As a general rule, it should never be the researcher's role to change any answers provided by respondents. However, there is an even bigger problem caused by changing verbal responses into numerical scales. It is not statistically valid, as illustrated by Figure 7.7.

Strictly speaking a numerical scale is known as interval scaling and it is statistically valid to average the scores given by customers because all the points on the scale assume roughly equal proportions in the respondent's mind. The distance between 5 and 4 is the same as the distance between 2 and

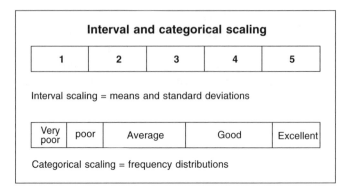

Figure 7.7 Interval and categorical scaling

3 etc. With a verbal type scale respondents have allocated their responses to a category. At best, a verbal scale will be ordinal in nature. We know that excellent is better than good, but we don't know how much better. Moreover, the points on a verbal scale do not assume equal proportions in respondents' minds, as shown in Figure 7.7. For these reasons it is only considered to be statistically valid to analyse categorical and ordinal scales using a frequency distribution like the one shown in Figure 7.5.

7.5 Reporting the results

7.5.1 Reporting numerical scales

7.5.1.1 Importance

Even if satisfaction preceded importance on the questionnaire, importance scores should always be reported first since understanding customers' priorities is the logical starting point. The hypothetical example used to illustrate the results in this section is from a typical supermarket survey. For clarity, only eight attributes are shown in the charts whereas in real life there would usually be fifteen to twenty customer requirements included on the questionnaire. Figure 7.8 shows the simplest way to report the results. The chart shows the average (i.e. the arithmetic mean) scores out of ten given by the respondents for the importance of each attribute.

The chart clearly demonstrates what matters most to customers. Average importance scores above nine indicate that the requirement is extremely important to customers. Those scoring above eight are important and above seven they are quite important. It is unusual to generate many average importance scores below seven in the main survey because only those items shown by the exploratory research to be important to customers should find their way onto

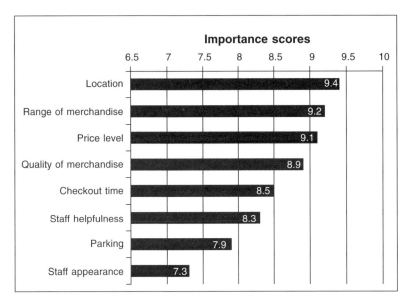

Figure 7.8 Importance scores

the questionnaire. It is interesting that in the surveys that we undertake for clients, attributes scoring only five or six for importance usually did not feature strongly in the exploratory research results but were included in the main survey at the request of the client, often because the client felt that they must be important to customers. Such attributes rarely score any higher for importance at the main survey stage across a much larger sample. It is true that suppliers often do not understand their customers as well as they think they do!

Two additional things should be noted about the chart shown in Figure 7.8. First, everything is listed in order of importance to the customer. The order in which the attributes were listed on the questionnaire is irrelevant for reporting. There is an important message for everybody here. '*These are the things that are important to customers and this is the order of priority.*' You should remain consistent and list everything in order of importance to the customer all the way through reporting the results.

Second, the scale on the chart does not go from 1 to 10. If it did all the bars would appear at first glance to be a very similar length and anybody who just skims the report may glance at it and conclude, '*that's not telling us anything, there's not much difference there.*' In reality there is a big difference in importance between an average score of 7 and one of 9. So it is always better to truncate the scale to highlight the differences and make sure you get the message across.

7.5.1.2 Satisfaction

Respondents will have scored the list of requirements for satisfaction as well as importance. Figure 7.9 shows the average scores for satisfaction. You can see that they are still listed in order of priority to the customer and still with the truncated scale to highlight the differences.

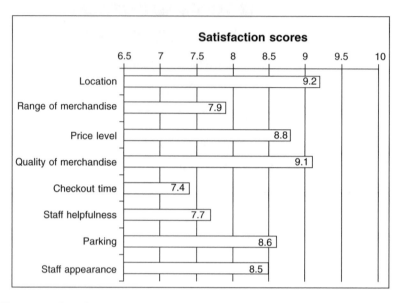

Figure 7.9 Satisfaction scores

Average satisfaction scores above nine on a ten-point scale show an extremely high level of customer satisfaction. Scores of eight equate to 'satisfied' customers, seven to 'quite satisfied' and six (which is only just above the mid-point of 5.5) to 'borderline' or 'much room for improvement'. Average satisfaction scores of five or lower are below the mid-point and suggest a considerable number of dissatisfied customers. Any attribute with an average satisfaction score below six should be treated very seriously. It would also be good practice in telephone surveys or personal interviews to probe all scores below 6 out of 10 given by respondents to elicit the reason for the customer's dissatisfaction. This will enable the research to explain any poor satisfaction scores such as 'checkout time' or 'staff helpfulness' in this example. Self-completion questionnaires can ask for comments for low satisfaction scores, but most respondents will not provide them and when they do the comments will often be quite brief.

As suggested earlier, standard deviations should be calculated for each satisfaction score because behind an apparently satisfactory score may be a group of customers who are extremely satisfied but some who are very unhappy. If so, you need to understand which types of customers are not being satisfied by your organisation. This may be shown by examining the scores for different segments, which helps to explain why you need a sufficiently large sample to provide statistically reliable sample sizes at segment level.

The satisfaction chart provides very interesting information, but the most useful outcomes can be produced when you put the importance and the satisfaction scores together and ask that very simple but absolutely fundamental question, '*are we doing best what matters most to customers?*'

7.5.1.3 Doing best what matters most

The answer to that question will be shown in Figure 7.10. By comparing the importance and satisfaction scores you can use 'gap analysis' to identify PFIs (priorities for improvement). Not rocket science, gap analysis indicates that if the satisfaction bar is shorter than the importance one the company may have a problem! But that is the main strength of the chart. It is clear, simple and obvious. Anybody in the organisation can look at it, understand it and draw the right conclusions.

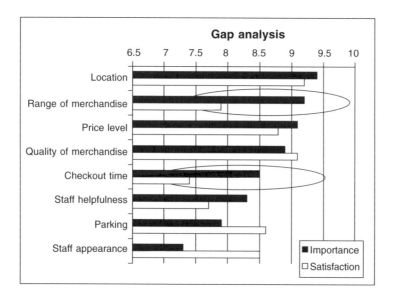

Figure 7.10 Gap analysis

Clearly, there are some areas, such as 'location' and 'quality of merchandise' where the organisation concerned is more or less meeting customers' requirements. There are some, such as 'staff appearance' where customers' requirements are being exceeded. Remembering the implication of the high standard deviation for the importance of parking, the organisation would be prudent not to assume it is exceeding customers' requirements on that attribute without checking the satisfaction scores for parking provided by the segment that thought parking was very important. Most importantly there are some attributes where the company is failing to meet customers' requirements and these are the ones it needs to focus on if it wants to improve customer satisfaction. These are the PFIs, the priorities for improvement. The bigger the gap, the bigger the problem, and you can see from Figure 7.10 that the biggest PFI, the area with the greatest potential for improving customer satisfaction is not the attribute with the lowest satisfaction score (quick checkout) but the one with the largest gap – range of merchandise.

7.5.1.4 The Satisfaction Index

After identifying the PFIs, the second major outcome to be produced from the data is an overall index of customer satisfaction, often called a Satisfaction Index or a Customer Satisfaction Index. There are several possible ways of producing such an index. You could include a catch all question at the end of the questionnaire such as:

And overall, how satisfied are you with the products and services of. . .?

or

And overall, how satisfied are you with your experience of. . .?

The trouble with this approach is that the more variables you ask people to consider when responding to a question, the less reliable the answer is, and there are a lot of variables in that overall satisfaction question. On reflection, you do not need to ask that catch all question because you have already asked each respondent about all the main things that make them satisfied or dissatisfied. A second approach would therefore be to calculate the overall average of all the satisfaction scores. That would be better, but it would not be ideal, because some things are more important to customers than others, and their most important requirements influence their satisfaction judgement more than things that are less important to them. An accurate Satisfaction Index therefore has to work in the same way. It has to be more strongly influenced by the attributes with the highest importance scores. In other words it must be a weighted average satisfaction score, which requires a two-step process for its calculation.

Calculating the weighting factors

The importance scores are used to calculate the weighting factors. The first column of data in Figure 7.11 shows the average importance scores from the supermarket example. To calculate the weighting factors simply total all the importance scores. In this example they add up to 68.6. Then express each one as a percentage of the total. Using 'staff appearance' as an example, 7.3 divided by 68.6, multiplied by 100 produces a weighting factor of 10.64%.

Calculating the Satisfaction Index

The second step is to multiply each satisfaction score by its corresponding

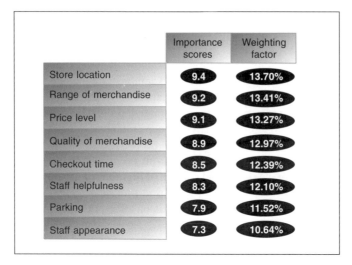

Figure 7.11 Calculating the weighting factors

weighting factor. The first column of data in Figure 7.12 shows all the average satisfaction scores and the second column of data shows the weighting factors that were calculated in Figure 7.11. Taking staff appearance as the example again, the satisfaction score of 8.5 multiplied by the weighting factor of 10.64% produces a weighted score of 0.9. The overall weighted average is determined by adding up all the weighted scores. In this example they add up

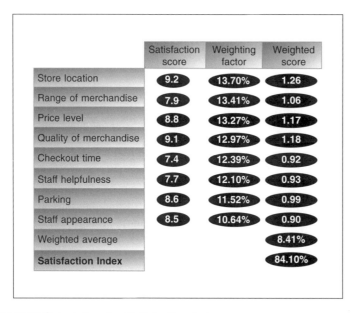

Figure 7.12 Calculating the Satisfaction Index

to 8.41, so the supermarket's weighted average satisfaction score is 8.41 out of 10. It is normal to convert that score into a percentage and say that the Satisfaction Index is 84.1%.

In this example, the Satisfaction Index shows that the supermarket is 84% successful in satisfying its customers. To demonstrate the mathematical basis of the formula, imagine that the supermarket was such a wonderful supplier that all the customers surveyed insisted on giving satisfaction scores of 10 out of 10 for every single one of the customer requirements. In that eventuality the average satisfaction scores would all be 10. The weighting factors would all stay the same because they come from the importance scores, and the weighted scores in the right-hand column of Figure 7.12 would all be different to each other, but they would all add up to precisely 10.0. That is how the formula works. Total customer satisfaction on all requirements would produce a Satisfaction Index of 100%.

Updating the Satisfaction Index

It is important that the Satisfaction Index is updateable. It has to provide you with a comparable measure of satisfaction that you can monitor in the years ahead even if the questions on your questionnaire have to change as customers' requirements change. Basically, the Satisfaction Index answers this question: '*How successful are we at satisfying our customers according to the 20 things that are most important to them?*' (Assuming 20 customer requirements on the questionnaire.)

If the questionnaire has to change in the future because customers' priorities have changed, the Satisfaction Index remains a measure of exactly the same thing.

> *How successful are we at satisfying our customers according to the 20 things that are most important to them?*

That comparability also applies for organisations with different customer groups who need to be asked different questions in the same year. Provided that the exploratory research has been correctly undertaken, the Satisfaction Indices from two or more surveys asking different questions are directly comparable.

7.5.2 Reporting verbal scales

As explained in Section 7.5.2, frequency distributions have to be used to analyse verbal scales. To make reporting simpler, a 'percentage satisfied' figure is often quoted. On the typical 5-point verbal scale this is often the sum of responses in the top two boxes. Using the frequency distribution shown in Figure 7.5, the top two box satisfaction scores would be as follows.

Opening hours	61%
Car parking	42%

Queue time	22%
Friendliness of staff	66%
Appearance of staff	84%

The obvious weakness of this approach is that it ignores three of the five sets of data that have been collected. For example, satisfaction with 'opening hours' looks reasonable, but it has the highest percentage of very dissatisfied customers, more even than 'queue times' where satisfaction is apparently much lower. It also ignores the mix of scores in the top two boxes. The organisation appears to be performing better on 'friendliness of staff' than on 'opening hours' but Figure 7.5 shows that more customers are 'very satisfied' with 'opening hours' than with 'friendliness of staff'. The 'courtesy four' is a phenomenon that is widely recognised amongst people who are experienced in customer satisfaction research. Where customers are broadly satisfied (which they are with most organisations), most tick the second box. Unfortunately, however, research from Harvard Business School amongst others, shows that the relationship between customer satisfaction and loyalty is often exponential. In other words, the relationship between satisfaction and loyalty is much stronger for top box scorers than for those (usually far more numerous), who tick the second box and are merely 'satisfied'. If a five-point scale has been used, the organisation would be well advised to focus only on top box scores. In the example given in Figure 7.5, the reported 'top box' results would now appear as follows:

Opening hours	34%
Car parking	16%
Queue time	4%
Friendliness of staff	32%
Appearance of staff	40%

Due to the statistical impossibility of generating mean scores from categorical or ordinal scales, there is no satisfactory way of producing a weighted average score for a Satisfaction Index. Companies using five-point verbal scales would typically average their reported satisfaction scores from all the requirements or report the result of an overall satisfaction question as their headline Satisfaction Index.

Gap analysis is also difficult. If a top two box approach is used, the scores for importance and satisfaction can be compared, but the absence of 60% of the scale will make this method a very blunt instrument. Although not ideal, it is probably better to base PFIs on the satisfaction scores alone if verbal scales are used.

7.6 Conclusions

(a) Since the introduction to ISO 9001:2000 specifies that organisations must focus on *'continual improvement of processes based on objective measurement'*, it will be necessary to formally survey customers rather than informally consult them during the normal course of business. Unless the organisation has a very small customer base, this will involve a quantitative survey with a sample of at least 100 and preferably 200 respondents.

(b) ISO 9001:2000 gives the organisation the responsibility for *'determination of applicable methods, including statistical techniques'*, and these have been explained in this chapter for both numerical and verbal scales.

(c) Unless samples are very small, data should be analysed by computer, probably using a standard spreadsheet package. Specialist software will be beneficial only to organisations conducting frequent surveys.

(d) Numerical scales should be analysed using means and standard deviations, with frequency distributions used for verbal scales. It is not valid to convert verbal responses to a numerical scale at the analysis stage.

(e) Examining the gaps between importance and satisfaction identifies priorities for improvement.

(f) A headline Satisfaction Index should be a weighted average satisfaction score. If exploratory research has been conducted and the questionnaire has been based on customers' main requirements, the Satisfaction Index will provide a measure of the organisation's success in meeting customers' requirements. Therefore, your Satisfaction Index will give a comparable trend measure in the years ahead even if the questions change as customers' requirements evolve. It will also be comparable across different surveys, which may ask different questions, such as different business units within your organisation.

8

Customer communication

Summary

There are various stages where communication with customers will be essential or helpful. The entire process of customer satisfaction measurement involves communicating with customers, from the exploratory research to identify customers' requirements through to the main survey itself. Even if the main survey is postal or web-based, it remains a customer communication process. These processes have already been covered in the preceding chapters of this book, but there are other aspects of customer communication that are important both to the survey process and to the bigger picture of continual improvement of customer satisfaction. There are three main areas of customer communication that will be covered in this chapter.

(a) How to introduce the survey to customers to maximise participation and to enhance customers' perception of the purpose and professionalism of the exercise.
(b) Providing feedback after the survey to inform customers about its results and the learning that your organisation has gained from the exercise.
(c) Continuing the communication on a regular basis to keep customers informed about the improvements your organisation is making as a consequence of the survey.

8.1 What the Standard says

The most fundamental aspect of communicating with customers applies to the process for measuring customer satisfaction. ISO 9000:2000 makes it quite clear that customer satisfaction can be measured and monitored only through communicating with customers. Beyond the actual measurement of satisfaction, however, the Standard does make specific reference to customer communication in Section 7. As we saw in Chapter 3, Section 7.2 of the Standard, '*Customer-related processes*', is mainly concerned with identifying customers' requirements, but the final clause, 7.2.3, is devoted to '*Customer communication*'. The very brief clause states:

The organisation shall determine and implement effective arrangements for communicating with customers in relation to

(a) product information,
(b) enquiries, contracts or order handling, including amendments, and
(c) customer feedback including customer complaints.

Communicating with customers about products, enquiries and orders is clearly a normal part of business. Providing feedback to customers on other aspects of their relationship with your organisation is less widely practised, but there is considerable evidence that communicating with customers about your organisation's efforts to understand and meet their requirements can be a very effective tool in the quest for continual improvement in customer satisfaction.

8.2 Introducing the survey to customers

As we stated when we looked at maximising response rates, the introductory letter has a very important role to play. As well as increasing the response rate it will also improve the quality of response by raising the perceived value of the exercise in customers' minds. Carrying out a customer survey also provides an opportunity to enhance the image of your organisation by demonstrating its customer focus, and the introductory letter will play an important role here. Conversely, carrying out a customer survey in an amateurish or thoughtless way could damage your reputation. Figure 8.1 summarises the three main aspects of introducing the survey and these concern whom to tell, what to tell them and how to tell them.

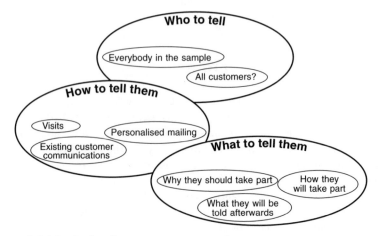

Figure 8.1 Introducing the survey – an overview

8.2.1 Who?

If you are serious about the CSM process there is only one answer to this question. You should inform all customers. Making sure that all customers know that you are committed to customer satisfaction and are prepared to invest to achieve it is a significant factor in making satisfaction gains. Instead of sitting back and hoping that customers will notice your efforts and commitment you should take control and make sure they do. Where organisations have a very large customer base, this communication may become costly. If budgets are not sufficient, the survey could be introduced to those sampled to participate, and communication to the entire customer base provided in the form of feedback after the survey.

8.2.2 How?

This will clearly depend on how many customers you have. If you have a very small number of customers in a business market it is most productive to explain the process personally to each one through well briefed customer contact staff. As the size of the customer base increases, a personal letter to each customer becomes the most feasible option. With a very large customer base a special mailing would be costly although it is worth considering its long-term effectiveness in building customer loyalty compared with a similar spend on advertising. If cost does rule out a special mailing you should consider the possibility of using existing communication channels to inform customers of your CSM programme. This may include printing a special leaflet to be enclosed with an existing mailing or creating space in an existing customer publication such as a newsletter.

8.2.3 What?

There are three things you need to tell them:

  (i) Why you are doing it.
 (ii) How you are going to do it.
(iii) The feedback you will provide afterwards.

8.2.3.1 The purpose of the survey

Don't assume that customers will correctly interpret the purpose of a CSM survey. Many people will react negatively to your initial approach to survey them. Think about it. Without an introductory letter, your telephone call or letter will arrive unexpectedly. You will never catch customers at a convenient time. They will almost always be busy doing something else and will certainly have more important issues on their mind than your survey. The most natural customer reaction is therefore to see your survey as an inconvenience at best, an intrusion at worst. After all, what's in it for them? The first purpose of your letter is to tell them. It may seem obvious, but point out that the purpose of the survey is to identify whether customers' requirements are being fully met so that action can be taken to improve customer satisfaction where necessary.

8.2.3.2 The survey details

Customers clearly need to know what form the survey will take. If the introductory letter accompanies a postal questionnaire it will include the instructions for completing and returning the questionnaire. If you undertake a telephone survey an introductory letter should give brief details of the topics that will be covered and should stress that an appointment will be made to interview customers at a time convenient to them. It is also useful at this point to reiterate how valuable the customer feedback is in order to encourage the highest possible participation rates.

8.2.3.3 Feedback

Research evidence suggests that promising feedback is the single most effective element in increasing response rates. The introductory letter (Figure 8.2) must therefore inform customers that they will receive feedback on the results and on the key issues that have been identified as a result of the survey. You should also promise to share with customers the actions that you plan to take to address any issues.

Introductory letter

Dear ......

As part of our ongoing commitment to customer service at XYZ, we are about to conduct a survey to measure customer satisfaction. I would therefore like to enlist your help in identifying those areas where we fully meet your needs and those where you would like to see improvements. We attach the utmost importance to this exercise since it is your feedback that will enable us to continually improve our service in order to meet your needs.

I believe that this process needs to be carried out in a professional manner and have therefore appointed The Leadership Factor Ltd, an agency that specialises in this work, to carry out the exercise on our behalf. They will contact you in the near future to arrange a convenient time for a telephone interview lasting approximately 15 minutes.

The Leadership Factor will treat your responses in total confidence and we will receive only an overall summary of the results of the interviews. Of course, if there are any particular points that you would like to draw to our attention you can ask for them to be recorded and your name associated with them if you wish.

After the survey we will provide you with a summary of the results and let you know what action we plan to take as a result of the findings. I regard this as a very important step in our aim of continually improving the level of service we provide to our customers and I would like to thank you in advance for helping us with your feedback.

Yours sincerely

XXXXXX
Chief Executive Officer

Figure 8.2 Sample introductory letter

8.3 Feedback on the survey results

Having promised feedback to customers in the introductory letter, the time has come to provide it. You now need to consider three things:

(i) Who should receive feedback?
(ii) What information is to be provided?
(iii) How it will be provided?

8.3.1 Who?

At the very least, feedback should be provided to all customers who took part in the survey. If the survey was an anonymous self-completion survey, you will not know who returned the questionnaires, in which case, it would not be possible to target feedback to respondents. If a telephone survey has been conducted, you would know which customers had participated even if their responses were confidential, so a thank you letter plus feedback could be provided to respondents. The key issue to consider is whether to go beyond respondents or those included in the original sample, and feed back the results to all customers. For organisations with a very large customer base the obvious answer is cost. The pertinent question, however, is whether the cost can be justified by the benefits.

8.3.1.1 Stimulating customer attitude change

Many organisations fail to realise the potential value of feeding back the CSM results to the entire customer base. We introduced the satisfaction improvement loop in Chapter 5. It demonstrates that before you can achieve gains in customer satisfaction, customers must first notice any improvements made by your organisation and second, modify their attitudes accordingly. Both of those steps are major hurdles to overcome. As far as the first is concerned, many organisations take it for granted that if they make improvements along the lines indicated by the customer survey customers will notice. That is a very dangerous assumption. Many customers will not, or, at best, only after repeated exposure. Once customers have noticed the changes, they will still have to modify their attitudes before they will feel more satisfied, and certainly before they will communicate that increased satisfaction to anyone else. Clearly, the more you can do to accelerate that process, the more effective your CSM programme will be. Providing feedback on the survey results and on the actions your organisation plans to take in response to the customers' views is a good step in the right direction. By working on the satisfaction improvement loop, you can, to an extent, 'talk up' customer satisfaction. Figure 8.3 shows the points on the satisfaction improvement loop where customer feedback can usefully be injected. Indeed, as we will see later in this chapter, where there are perception gaps, talking up customer satisfaction

Figure 8.3 Accelerating the satisfaction improvement process

is the only way to improve it. Consequently, there is an opportunity to improve customers' perception of your organisation by providing information on the survey results to the entire customer base.

8.3.2 What?

The starting point is to produce a short feedback report. This should include a summary of the results followed by an outline of the key issues arising from the survey. The key issues will usually be the PFIs, but it is unwise to refer to them as PFIs in the feedback report since the terminology might suggest that your organisation has too much improving to do! 'Key issues', or 'survey outcomes' is therefore more suitable wording. Having communicated the results you need to tell customers what action will be taken as a result of their feedback and when it is going to be taken. This may seem like a bold commitment, but if the goal is to improve customer satisfaction, action will have to be taken anyway. Informing customers that it is going to be taken is the first step in improving their perception and accelerating the satisfaction improvement loop.

One of the most difficult decisions for organisations to take is the level of detail to go into when providing feedback on the survey results to customers. One option is to feed back the results exactly as they are, as shown in Figure 8.4.

This chart would not be the same as those used internally. There is no need to feed back importance scores to customers, and satisfaction scores should be presented in questionnaire order (which was presumably a logical order) rather than in order of importance, which will not seem logical in the absence of importance scores. Also note that the scale is not shortened. This has the effect of making even the lowest satisfaction scores appear much better than they do when the scale is truncated as in Figure 7.9.

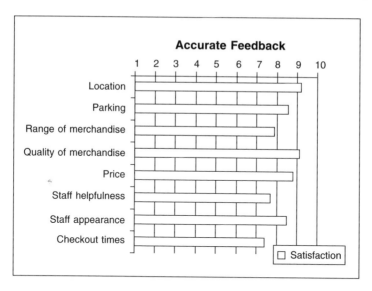

Figure 8.4 Accurate feedback

Some organisations feel very uneasy about providing the actual scores, perhaps through fear that they may fail to improve the following year or, in some close knit industrial markets, that the information might fall into the hands of a competitor. To alleviate such concerns, an alternative is to provide indicative feedback, using symbols or general descriptions to suggest levels of satisfaction.

Although it is understandable why some organisations worry about feeding back the exact scores, indicative feedback can be more damaging. Symbols and general descriptions will often look worse than the real scores, as is the case with Figures 8.4 and 8.5. Moreover, if customers form the conclusion

	Customer Requirement	Satisfaction
1st	Location	☺
2nd	Range of merchandise	☹
3rd	Price	☺
4th	Quality of merchandise	☺
5th	Checkout times	☹
6th	Staff helpfulness	☹
7th	Parking	😐
8th	Staff appearance	😐

Figure 8.5 Indicative feedback

that the results have been massaged in an attempt to disguise poor performance, their impression of the organisation could be adversely affected.

8.3.3 How?

How the information is provided depends mainly on the size of the customer base. Personal presentation is by far the most effective method and is quite feasible for companies with a fairly small number of key accounts. For a medium sized customer base, a copy of the feedback report should be mailed with a personalised letter. If very large numbers of customers are involved, mass-market communications will need to be used. These might include a company newsletter or a brief survey report mailed with another customer communication such as a bill. Retailers and other organisations whose customers visit them can cost-effectively utilise point-of-sale material. This may include posters, leaflets, display cards or stands. Moreover, customer contact staff can be briefed to support the feedback drive through their verbal communications with customers. Point of sale displays might, for example, encourage customers to ask staff for further details. Even TV advertising has been used to communicate to very large customer bases the survey results and the fact that action is being taken.

8.4 Progress reports

The final hurdle of the satisfaction improvement loop is the fact that even after they have noticed your improvements, customers still have to change their attitudes, before a satisfaction gain will be achieved. Although people can form attitudes quickly, they tend to change them slowly, but it is possible to speed up customers' attitude change and improve satisfaction by providing updates on action that has been taken, preferably at least twice between annual surveys. This will be particularly effective when low satisfaction scores are caused by 'perception gaps'.

8.4.1 Performance and perception gaps

Where organisations receive poor satisfaction scores for individual attributes, these may be explained as a 'performance gap' or a 'perception gap'. To illustrate, imagine a company received a poor average satisfaction score for 'on time delivery'. This could be a 'performance gap', meaning that they really are very poor at delivery – they do not keep their delivery promises, they are always arriving late and always letting customers down. Faced with such a performance gap, the only way the company would be able to increase customer satisfaction would be to improve its delivery reliability.

On the other hand, it might have received a poor average satisfaction score for 'on time delivery' and yet know that its delivery performance is very good. The organisation might even monitor it and have computer print-outs showing delivery reliability at very high levels for the last year. However, the organisation may have experienced problems earlier (maybe as much as two or three years ago), perhaps as a result of installing a new computer system. True, there were some real delivery problems then, but that was all resolved nearly 2 years ago. Not in the customers' minds it wasn't! Customers can remember bad things that suppliers do to them for a very long time, and if improvements are made, but customers' attitudes remain focused on the bad times, you end up with 'perception gaps'.

If the organisation has a perception gap it can't improve customer satisfaction by improving its performance. In the 'on time delivery' example that has already been done. It can improve satisfaction only by demonstrating to customers how good its performance really is and consequently hope to change customers' attitudes. That is a customer communication task and illustrates why customer feedback is so important. The customer feedback straight after the survey can start off the process. In the example quoted, the company could acknowledge 'on time delivery' as a key issue arising from the survey and tell customers that it is taking the matter very seriously and will report back on progress on a regular basis.

We have seen many cases of perception gaps and how they have been successfully overcome by customer feedback. One client of ours in an industrial market had exactly this type of perception gap for on time delivery. They informed customers that they were going to set targets for delivery reliability, monitor their performance against those targets every month and feed back the results to customers. (In fact, they were already monitoring the delivery reliability but it doesn't do any harm for customers to think that it had been introduced as a result of the customer survey.)

Every month for the next year they sent a fax to every customer plotting their delivery reliability against target and highlighting how many of the customer's own deliveries that month were on time or late. Since delivery reliability had already been improved, the customers' faxes would show 100% reliability for their own deliveries almost every month. One year later when the customer survey was updated, the score for on time delivery had improved significantly even though the delivery performance had not changed at all!

8.5 Conclusions

(a) Clause 7.2.3 of ISO 9001:2000 makes a specific reference to customer communication. Although most of the brief clause covers everyday aspects of customer communication, the clause does suggest that customer feedback should be provided.

(b) As far as customer satisfaction measurement is concerned, a key customer communication is the letter that introduces the survey to customers. A professional introductory letter will improve the response rate and the quality of response.

(c) Providing customer feedback after the survey is even more important. It is essential to provide it to those who have participated but there are benefits in providing post-survey feedback to all customers since it demonstrates that your organisation is customer focused and is committed to taking action to improve customer satisfaction.

(d) There is much evidence from customer satisfaction research that customer communication can be an effective element in continual improvement of customer satisfaction especially where there are perception gaps.

9

Internal communication

Summary

Good internal communication is increasingly seen as the essential lubricant for the smooth working of organizations across all areas of operation. This particularly applies to any programme designed to improve customer satisfaction. ISO 9001:2000 recognises the importance of internal communication and makes it a responsibility of senior management. In this chapter we will explain how internal communications can be effectively used to:

(a) Gain employee buy-in to the customer satisfaction measurement process.
(b) Identify the extent to which employees understand customers' requirements and their ability to satisfy customers.
(c) Provide feedback to employees on the results of the survey as a precursor to taking effective action.

9.1 What the Standard says

ISO 9001:2000 makes internal communication one of the responsibilities of top management. This is specified right at the beginning of the *'Management responsibility'* section in clause 5.1, *'Management commitment'*.

> Top management shall provide evidence of its commitment to the development and implementation of the quality management system and continually improving its effectiveness by
>
> (a) communicating to the organisation the importance of meeting customer as well as statutory and regulatory requirements.

This theme is developed in clause 5.5.2:

> Top management shall appoint a member of management who, irrespective of other responsibilities, shall have responsibility and authority that includes
>
> (c) ensuring the promotion of awareness of customer requirements throughout the organisation.

According to clause 5.5.3:

> *Top management shall ensure that appropriate communication channels are established within the organisation and that communication takes place regarding the effectiveness of the quality management system.*

Although this clause refers to the whole quality management system, one of its chief objectives is continual improvement in customer satisfaction. Leading practitioners of customer satisfaction measurement have known for many years that thorough internal feedback of survey results is the essential precursor to an effective satisfaction improvement programme. Whilst the Standard is quite right to suggest that feedback should also be provided on wider aspects of the quality management system, customer satisfaction should form a significant part of it.

ISO 9004:2000 gives more detail in clause 5.5.3 about how internal feedback might be provided. It recommends:

> *The management of the organisation should define and implement an effective and efficient process for communicating the quality policy, requirements, objectives and accomplishments. . . Activities for communicating include*
>
> *– management-led communication in work areas*
> *– team briefings and other meetings such as recognition of achievement*
> *– notice boards, in-house journals/magazines*
> *– audio-visual and electronic media, such as email and web sites*
> *– employee surveys and suggestion schemes.*

The suggestions apply equally well to customer survey feedback as they do to wider feedback on the performance of the quality management system. The most appropriate media will vary by organisation but ISO 9004:2000 is right to emphasise the value of involving employees whether through surveys, suggestion schemes or any other means. Employees will be at the heart of the organisation's ability to improve customer satisfaction. The more they buy into the importance of meeting customers' requirements, the more successful the organisation will be in continually improving customer satisfaction.

9.2 Employee buy-in

Ensuring employee buy-in should start right at the beginning. This step is frequently overlooked or performed inadequately by management. Employees need to know:

- why the customer survey is taking place;
- when it will happen;
- how it will be done;

- how to respond to customers if asked about it;
- how employees will be involved;
- what will happen after the survey.

The ideal way to achieve these internal communication objectives is to organise a formal launch of the customer satisfaction measurement process.

9.2.1 The launch

If your organisation is introducing customer satisfaction measurement for the first time (or re-introducing it after some years), it is worth investing in a high profile launch attended by as many employees as possible. This can be built into an event with refreshments and maybe even some entertainment. The CEO must play a prominent part in the launch, as should the Quality Manager, other senior managers and the member of staff or the external agency who will be responsible for conducting the survey. A high profile launch will show the organisation and its senior managers walking the talk as far as customer satisfaction is concerned and, if done professionally will make a big impact on employees, far greater than memos, notices or even team briefings. A formal launch would not be appropriate for update surveys, but communications like team briefings, posters, notice boards and employee newsletters should be used. A key factor for updates as well as first time surveys is *management-led communication*. Senior management must demonstrate their full commitment to customer satisfaction and their belief that the measurement system will play a strong part in the organisation's continual improvement process.

As well as personally walking the talk, leaders will ensure that all aspects of the organisation constantly remind employees that their main purpose is to deliver customer satisfaction. As we pointed out in Chapter 1, MBNA have a daily customer satisfaction measure and a quarterly bonus that builds up each day that the measure is over target. They also have a catch phrase, 'think of yourself as a customer', which is engrained into employees from their first day with the company. They are also constantly reminded about it since it is woven into all the carpets and is featured above every doorway in the building.

9.2.2 Key staff

Whilst all employees need to know about the survey and believe in its value as a continual improvement tool, some key managers will need a higher level of buy-in. This will include senior management and any managers and staff who will be responsible for implementing the survey findings. In business-to-business markets the sales force, especially in the field, should also be seen as key staff. There are three ways of ensuring key staff buy in:

- The CEO must be seen to be the strongest champion of customer focus and customer satisfaction measurement within the organisation.

- Key staff should have a significant input into the process, especially at the exploratory stage, where the survey methodology and the type of information provided at the end of the survey will be determined. Unless key staff buy into the process at the beginning there is a considerable danger that they won't buy into it at the end, especially when it is producing recommendations that will increase their workload!
- Involve key staff in providing internal feedback after the survey (see 9.4).

Understanding the principle that the survey must be based on the lens of the customer rather than the lens of the organisation is a very important start, but they must also be given an opportunity to contribute at the design stage. Key staff should therefore be invited to review the proposed methodology, make suggestions and have any queries answered. They should also have an input into the exploratory research. Although the purpose of the exploratory research is to understand the lens of the customer, the focus group facilitator or depth interviewer does need a comprehensive list of factors that may be important to customers to use as prompts if necessary. Key staff should be involved in suggesting items for that list. If they are involved in this way, nobody will be able to suggest that an important factor was overlooked by the exploratory research.

9.3 The mirror survey

While carrying out a customer survey it can be extremely beneficial to survey employees at the same time as customers to identify 'understanding gaps' – areas where staff do not properly understand what is important to customers or fail to realise that the level of service they provide is not good enough. This exercise is known as a mirror survey and it involves administering a slightly modified version of the customer questionnaire to employees. Exactly the same attributes should be measured but you will effectively ask your staff:

How important or unimportant do you think these things are to our customers?

And:

How satisfied or dissatisfied do you think customers are with our performance in these areas?

A mirror survey is normally conducted at the same time as the main survey. It is based on a self-completion questionnaire, which should be given out and collected back in from employees to achieve the highest possible response rate. By highlighting understanding gaps the mirror survey may help to pinpoint the causes of any customer dissatisfaction. A sample questionnaire for a mirror survey is shown in Appendix 3.

9.3.1 Understanding customers' requirements

Using the same results for the supermarket that we saw earlier, the chart in Figure 9.1 shows the difference between the customers' average score for the importance of each attribute and the average score given by employees. Alarm bells should sound when employees underestimate the importance of a customer requirement. The chart shows that employees significantly underestimate the importance of checkout time, scoring it 0.7 lower than customers.

Figure 9.1 Customers' priorities – the employees' view

9.3.2 Understanding customer satisfaction

The second mirror survey chart, shown in Figure 9.2 shows the difference in average scores for satisfaction given by customers and employees. There may be a problem where employees overestimate their success in satisfying customers. The chart shows that they do that with checkout time. The average satisfaction score given by employees was 1.2 higher than the one given by customers. It is easy to imagine the kind of understanding gap that could occur here. The employees may be completing the questionnaire and thinking:

We're pretty good on checkout time. As soon as there are 4 customers in a line, we rush over and open a new till.

Meanwhile, customers in the stores are thinking:

What dreadful service. There are already 3 people in this queue and they still haven't opened another check-out.

Figure 9.2 Customer satisfaction – the employees' view

9.3.3 The value of mirror surveys

As well as highlighting understanding gaps on specific attributes, a mirror survey will sometimes highlight a much deeper malaise in the organisation. Whilst some organisations have an incredibly accurate understanding of customers' needs and perceptions, others can display a woeful understanding across the board. In these latter cases, the mirror survey has identified a significant staff training need since the organisation will never satisfy its customers until its staff understand what they must do to achieve customer satisfaction. Sometimes, when employees give satisfaction scores that are consistently higher than those given by customers, a degree of unhealthy complacency can be identified. However, the opposite can also happen, where employees give significantly lower satisfaction scores than customers for all the attributes. This can be a sign of poor staff morale, sometimes based on too many years of criticism by management for their poor performance.

Even if the mirror survey does not identify any understanding gaps or highlight any wider problems within the organisation, completing the questionnaire is a very tangible way of involving employees in the CSM process and making them think about the issues of importance to customers. Once the results have been analysed, employees find it very interesting to compare their scores with those given by customers and that added interest helps to facilitate the internal feedback process.

9.4 Internal feedback

Feeding back the results to employees is an essential element in the long-term health of a CSM programme. Little action will be taken to improve customer satisfaction if employees don't know enough about the results or their implications. The extent of the feedback provided to employees will also send messages about how important the customer survey is to the organisation. So rather than providing superficial feedback through newsletters, notice boards or e-mail, the results should be personally presented in the form of feedback workshops, preferably to all employees but at least to all those who have an important role in delivering customer satisfaction. It is true that for larger organisations, face-to-face feedback workshops for all or a significant proportion of employees will be quite a costly exercise. If some people in the organisation question the wisdom of that investment it is not difficult to quantify the cost of the workshops in terms of staff pay or lost production. Any opponents of the feedback workshops can then be asked whether improving customer satisfaction is worth that investment to the organisation. With a little more difficulty it would be possible to calculate the extent to which customer loyalty would have to increase to justify that investment, and you will find, almost without exception, that the required increase would be extremely small.

A suggested agenda for an internal feedback workshop is shown in Figure 9.3. The workshop should start by demonstrating that the survey was professionally conducted and therefore provides a reliable measure – in short that the right questions were asked to the right people. It is therefore important to explain the exploratory research that led to the design of a suitable questionnaire plus the robustness of the sample.

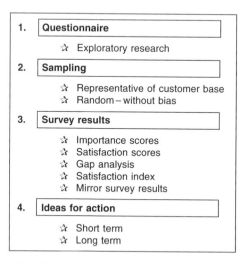

Figure 9.3 Internal feedback agenda

The results should then be presented – the importance scores, the satisfaction scores, the gap analysis and the Satisfaction Index. It is necessary to explain how the index is calculated and what it means, otherwise it will be perceived as little more than another dubious number invented by management. The mirror survey will generate added interest at this stage. Employees will be very interested to compare their own perceptions with those of customers. You can even inject some added excitement into proceedings by having one or more prizes for the employee(s) displaying the closest understanding of customers.

Finally you should look to the future. Start by reiterating the importance of the PFIs and then take the opportunity to invite ideas about how they might be addressed. Time permitting, it is very useful to break employees into small groups to discuss the issues. Ask them to brainstorm ways in which the PFIs could be addressed. Having generated a list of ideas, they should be sorted into two categories, ideas that could be implemented easily, quickly and at low cost (the quick wins) and those that are longer term, on grounds of cost or difficulty. They should then select the ones they consider to be their best three short-term and best three long-term ideas, and be prepared to present their suggestions to the rest of the workshop. This will result in a large number of ideas for action. The selection process can be taken a step further by asking everybody to score the full list of ideas in order to identify the best overall short-term and long-term ideas. Apart from the fact that employees, who are close to the action, will often think of good ideas which would not have occurred to management, the great advantage of this approach is that employees are far more likely to enthusiastically embrace a service improvement programme which they have helped to shape rather than one which has simply been handed down by management.

9.5 Conclusions

(a) Under ISO 9001:2000, internal communication is a responsibility of senior management.

(b) Internal communications should cover the effectiveness of the entire quality management system, but customer satisfaction is a very important part of the system and there is a specific responsibility to inform employees about customers' requirements.

(c) To succeed in continually improving customer satisfaction, the organisation must ensure employee buy-in. This should be done through a high profile launch when customer satisfaction measurement is first introduced into the organisation.

(d) Key staff need even greater levels of buy-in, to the methodology and to the customer requirements that will be included on the questionnaire. It is important that key staff are given the opportunity to contribute their views on customers' requirements before the exploratory research takes place.

(e) Another way of involving employees in the process is to conduct a mirror survey, which may also identify training needs based on understanding gaps.

(f) After the survey it is essential to introduce an effective process to feed back the results to employees. Workshops are much more effective than less personal media and will often generate ideas for addressing the PFIs.

10

ISO 9004:2000: Beyond customer satisfaction measurement

Summary

The first nine chapters of this book have covered everything that organisations need to understand to comply with the customer satisfaction measurement requirements of ISO 9001:2000. This chapter provides some thoughts about how organisations can go beyond that and focuses on four main areas:

(a) The new customer satisfaction related concepts introduced by ISO 9004:2000.
(b) Benchmarking customer satisfaction across industries.
(c) Monitoring competitors.
(d) Characteristics of organisations that are most successful at satisfying customers.

10.1 What the Standard says

As we saw earlier in this book, the fundamental purpose of the quality management system is to demonstrate the organisation's ability to consistently meet customers' requirements and focus the organisation's quest for continual improvement. This is emphasised right at the beginning of ISO 9001:2000 in clause 1.1 on the general scope of the Standard.

This International Standard specifies requirements for a quality management system where an organisation:

(a) Needs to demonstrate its ability to consistently provide product that meets customer and applicable regulatory requirements, and
(b) Aims to enhance customer satisfaction through the effective application of the system, including processes for the continual improvement of

the system and the assurance of conformity to customer and applicable regulatory requirements.

ISO 9001:2000 specifies the essential requirements of a quality management system capable of meeting the objectives outlined above. As we have seen throughout this book, customer satisfaction measurement is one of the important elements of such a quality management system. However, although customer satisfaction measurement is an essential prerequisite of an effective continual improvement system, it is not sufficient in itself. The most successful organisations will be those that most effectively use customer satisfaction and other management information to drive improvement in the business. This will require a quality management system that goes beyond the requirements of ISO 9001:2000 and into areas covered by ISO 9004:2000. In the first paragraph of its introduction, ISO 9004:2000 introduces some additional concepts.

The purpose of an organisation is:

(a) To identify and meet the needs and expectations of its customers and other interested parties (people in the organisation, suppliers, owners, society), to achieve competitive advantage, and to do this in an effective and efficient manner, and

(b) To achieve, maintain and improve overall organisational performance and capabilities.

It then goes on to list some advantages of this approach, similar to those mentioned in the first chapter of this book, including:

- *customer loyalty*
- *repeat business and referral*
- *operational results such as revenue and market share*
- *competitive advantage.*

10.1.1 Interested parties

Two important new areas are raised by the extracts from ISO 9004:2000 shown above. The first is the concept of interested parties. It is now widely recognised that the organisations that are most successful at satisfying customers tend to also have good and stable relationships with other stakeholders such as employees and shareholders. Harvard Business School calls this the 'customer–employee satisfaction mirror'. Many organisations have identified a close relationship between employee satisfaction and customer satisfaction. This includes McDonalds, Rank Xerox, MCI, Sears, plus several banks and utilities. The focus of this book is customers, not employees or other stakeholders, but ISO 9004:2000 is absolutely correct to recommend that to maximise their success, organisations have to meet the requirements of more groups than just customers. We would certainly recommend conducting employee satisfaction surveys and the principles of measuring satisfaction outlined in this book also apply to satisfaction surveys of other stakeholders whether internal customers, employees or members of the local community.

10.1.2 Competitive advantage

The second key concept introduced at the beginning of ISO 9004:2000 is competitive advantage. Meeting customers' requirements and having satisfied customers are commendable achievements, but they may not be enough to ensure success in the marketplace if one or more competitors exceeds customers' requirements and has very satisfied customers. The concept of competitive advantage will be more important to some organisations than to others, but those in a very competitive marketplace would be well advised to consider adopting some of the ideas suggested in ISO 9004:2000 and developed in this chapter. The introduction of ISO 9004:2000 goes on to say:

To satisfy customer and end user needs and expectations, the management of the organisation should

– understand the needs and expectations of its customers, including those of potential customers
– determine key product characteristics for its customers and end users
– identify and assess competition in its market
– identify market opportunities, weaknesses and future competitive advantage.

Section 5 on management responsibility is much more detailed in ISO 9004:2000. In the section on planning, clause 5.4.1 covers *'Quality objectives'* and includes more references to competitors.

The objectives should be capable of being measured in order to facilitate an efficient and effective review by management. When establishing these objectives, management should also consider

– levels of satisfaction of interested parties
– benchmarking, competitor analysis, opportunities for improvement.

As we know from earlier in this book, Section 8 of the Standard covers *'Measurement, analysis, improvement'*. ISO 9004:2000 goes into more detail here too. One of its paragraphs, clause 8.2.1.2 is entitled *'Measurement and monitoring of customer satisfaction'* and states:

Measurement and monitoring of customer satisfaction is based on review of customer related information. The collection of such information may be active or passive. Management should recognise that there are many sources of customer related information and should establish effective and efficient processes to collect, analyse and use this information for improving the performance of the organisation. The organisation should identify sources of customer and end user information, available in written and verbal forms, from internal and external sources. Examples of customer related information include:

- *customer and user surveys*
- *feedback on aspects of product*
- *customer requirements and contract information*
- *market needs*
- *service delivery data*
- *information relating to competition.*

In this final chapter of the book we will develop ideas of benchmarking and competitive analysis suggested by ISO 9004:2000.

10.2 Benchmarking your performance

Satisfaction Indexes are directly comparable since they simply measure the organisation's success in meeting its customers' requirements – whatever those requirements are. Provided exploratory research has been conducted and the questionnaire is based on customers' main requirements, it is perfectly feasible to compare performance across a large number and a wide variety of organisations. Our company has a large database of CSM results, enabling us to continually update a 'league table' that puts any individual result into context against other organisations.

In the little example we used in Chapter 7, our supermarket achieved a Satisfaction Index of 84.1%, but is that any good? Actually, it is very good, as shown in Figure 10.1, which gives an overview of the range of scores achieved by different organisations. The supermarket's Satisfaction Index of 84.1% is well above average.

The league table ranges from a small number of excellent organisations that can achieve a Satisfaction Index above 90%, down to an even smaller number who can only manage around 50%. Not surprisingly, these latter organisations are serving customers who have no choice of alternative supplier. As a general guide, you can interpret your Satisfaction Index as follows:

90%	Excellent
85%	Very good
80%	Good
75%	Borderline
70%	Cause for concern
65%	Poor
60%	Very poor

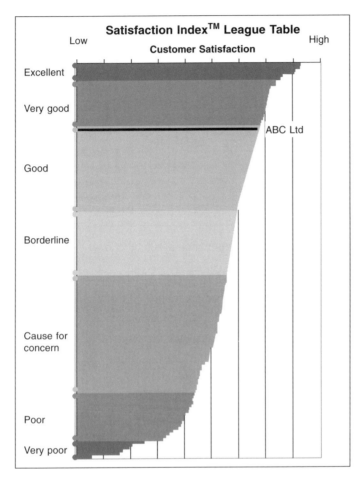

Figure 10.1 Satisfaction benchmark league table

Even more important than whether your Satisfaction Index is above average or below average is why you are in that position. Part of the answer will be found in your comparison against other organisations at an individual attribute level. There may be one key attribute where your performance is weaker than that of other organisations. Figure 10.2 shows how a fictitious company compares against the average scores of all other organisations across each of the attributes on its questionnaire.

Increasingly it is recognised that only the best is good enough, so you need to be able to benchmark your organisation against the best for each attribute, not just the average, as shown in Figure 10.3.

Our company, The Leadership Factor, can provide satisfaction benchmark comparisons.

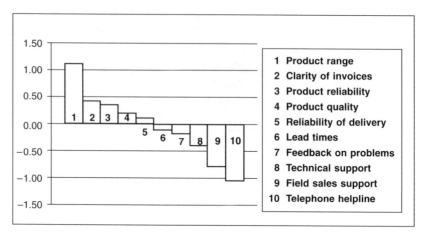

Figure 10.2 Comparative performance at attribute level

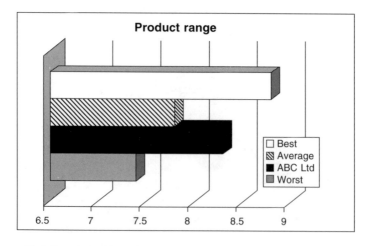

Figure 10.3 Benchmarking against the best

10.3 Comparisons with direct competitors

To make comparisons with direct competitors you need to collect your own data by extending the scope of your CSM survey. There are two main ways of generating the comparisons.

10.3.1 Comparison indicator

A simple and effective way of gaining an understanding of your position against competitors is to add a basic question to your questionnaire such as:

*Compared with similar stores / restaurants / venues / hotels that you visit,
would you say that XYZ Ltd is:*

> *The best*
> *Better than most*
> *About the same as most*
> *Worse than most*
> *The worst.*

This will provide the type of data shown in Figure 10.4 which can form the
basis for a very clear 'comparison indicator' to monitor over the years.

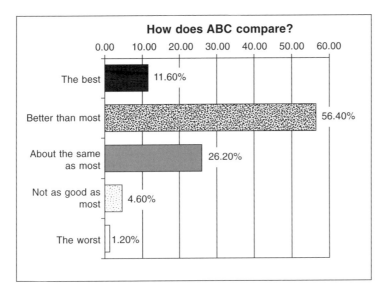

Figure 10.4 General comparison indicator

10.3.2 Market standing

Gaining more precise information on how you compare with direct competitors
can be acquired only by extending your CSM study into a full market standing
survey. There are two differences between this exercise and the process described
in this book. First, the sample frame (the population from which the sample
is drawn) must comprise all the buyers of the product or service in question
and not just your own customers or even your own contacts. Clearly, to get a
reliable view of how you compare against competitors you must survey all
shades of opinion, from your best friends to your worst enemies. Acquiring,
or, if necessary, compiling such a comprehensive sampling frame is critical
for the subsequent validity of the exercise and can be a lengthy process.

Second, the satisfaction section of the questionnaire must be extended to
generate scores for all the suppliers with whom that respondent is familiar.

Not all respondents will be able to give scores for all competitors, so you will end up with different sample sizes for each one. Consequently, for a market standing survey a larger sample size is almost always necessary since you need a reliable sample for the smallest competitor against whom you want a reliable comparison.

Strictly speaking, the scores given for competing suppliers on a market standing survey are performance scores rather than satisfaction scores. In many markets, people use only one supplier so would be able to express satisfaction or dissatisfaction only with that one supplier whose product and service they experience personally. For example, most people use only one bank, drive only one car, have only one mobile phone, etc. They may be familiar with several of the competing suppliers and have attitudes about how good their product or service is, whether their prices are competitive and how they perform on a range of criteria. For example, although you may use only one or two supermarkets, you probably have perceptions of others based on past experience, word of mouth, supplier advertising, general media profile, etc. Many people's perceptions of competing suppliers may be based on experiences that are very out of date, but it is on those perceptions that they are basing their supplier selection decisions.

From the data you can make a direct comparison with all competitors across each customer requirement, as shown in Figure 10.5.

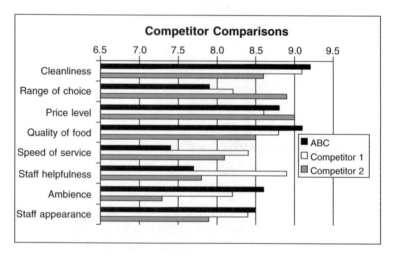

Figure 10.5 Competitor comparisons at attribute level

Using the same process as described for calculating the Satisfaction Index, you can work out the weighted average satisfaction scores for each supplier to produce a market standing chart as shown in Figure 10.6. Of course, to calculate a weighted average score, you will need to collect importance scores as well as performance scores for each requirement.

Clearly, the market standing survey provides extremely useful competitor

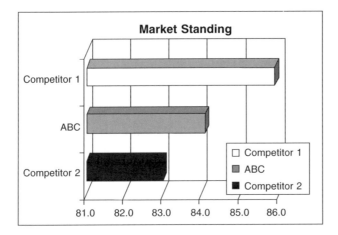

Figure 10.6 Market standing chart

intelligence but the research to produce it reliably will be considerably more extensive and expensive than a survey of your own customers. Moreover, even with the more detailed data generated by a market standing survey, the wider comparisons against other organisations described in the early part of this chapter remain important, for two reasons. First, customers will often form their judgement of your organisation by comparing you with the full range of organisations that they deal with, not just with your direct competitors (with whom they may have no dealings). Second, even if a market standing survey heralds you as better than your direct competitors, you may be operating in a market where all the suppliers are delivering a relatively poor level of service.

10.4 Achieving customer satisfaction

Knowing how you compare against other organisations on overall customer satisfaction and on performance at attribute level provides an essential basis for making improvements but it still does not explain why some organisations are more successful than others at making those improvements and achieving a high level of customer satisfaction. Tom Peters provided a very strong clue in his book *A Passion for Excellence*. A relevant passage is shown in Figure 10.7.

Our experience from working with a large number of organisations on customer satisfaction has highlighted a number of characteristics that are shared by the most successful ones, and these are summarised in Figure 10.8.

10.4.1 Top management support

The first and most important characteristic of organisations near the top of the

"Customer satisfaction is measured frequently. Sampling is extensive. Surveys are quantitative as well as qualitative (i.e. delivery times and feelings count equally); *the measures are taken very, very seriously. They are reviewed unfailingly by top management:* the development of such measures is taken as seriously as the development of budgetary measures or product reliability measures. Evaluation of people in all functions at all levels is significantly affected by the satisfaction measures"

Tom Peters
A Passion for Excellence

Figure 10.7 Top US companies and customer satisfaction

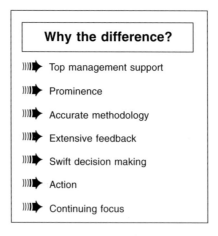

Figure 10.8 Characteristics of companies achieving high levels of satisfaction

satisfaction benchmark league table is a very high level of top management support and commitment. They do not just pay lip service to customer satisfaction but make it quite clear from their actions that satisfying customers really is a top priority of their organisation. We have spoken in this book about senior managers walking the talk. This is most clearly demonstrated when difficult budgetary decisions have to be taken. Are additional resources made available to provide extra staff when the customer survey shows a problem with service levels, or does top management simply encourage customer contact staff to try harder? When the American Customer Satisfaction Index showed falling customer satisfaction over a two-year period in the late 1990s, the main reason given for the decline was the detrimental effect on service levels caused by suppliers' cost cutting.

10.4.2 Prominence

In companies where customer satisfaction is a top priority, the customer survey process and the results are given very high prominence throughout the organisation. All possible methods of communication are used to provide information about the CSM process, including e-mail, staff newsletters, team briefing, notice boards, large posters on walls and special workshops. We have already referred to the 'think of yourself as a customer' slogans in the carpets and above the doorways at MBNA.

10.4.3 Accurate methodology

Organisations that are serious about customer satisfaction use the most accurate methodology they can when measuring it. You will not find them conducting a postal survey and ignoring the problem of non-response bias if they get low response rates. You will not find them drawing conclusions on ridiculously small sample sizes. You will not find them using their own members of staff (such as sales people) to interview customers that they know personally. A measure of customer satisfaction of dubious reliability is probably worse than no measure at all. Successful companies realise this and are prepared to invest in a robust methodology.

10.4.4 Extensive feedback

Companies at the top of the league table are not afraid of sharing their customer satisfaction results with customers as well as with employees. They know that providing extensive internal feedback is the essential pre-cursor to effective staff involvement in the service improvement process. They also understand that customers' attitudes change only slowly, even when customer service is improving, so they accelerate that process by providing customers with information on improvements they have made. Providing feedback is probably one of the biggest differentiators between the better and poorer performing suppliers and we covered that topic extensively in Chapters 8 and 9.

10.4.5 Swift decision making

Once a customer survey has been completed, all the information required to make decisions on improving customer satisfaction is available. No more will emerge by delaying things. On the contrary, customers' expectations may be changing and their satisfaction will certainly be declining if problems remain unresolved. The most effective organisations build decision making into their CSM project plan. They schedule a senior management meeting within days of the survey completion date and a process for cascading those decisions (often along with wider feedback of the survey results) a few days later.

10.4.6 Action

Clearly, all the measuring, the reporting, the decision making, and the feedback must lead to action. The whole point of conducting a CSM survey is to improve customer satisfaction and that will be achieved only through taking action on the PFIs. At least the use of a good CSM methodology will provide clear and credible evidence as to what the PFIs are. Some organisations, however, are far more effective at taking action than others. This is not a book on how to implement management decisions, but the ability to do so is an important differentiator between organisations at opposing ends of the satisfaction benchmark league table.

10.4.7 Continuing focus

Senior management must beware of adhering religiously to the first six steps in this section and then moving their attention onto other things. Improving customer satisfaction is very much 'a journey not a destination' and the company must be constantly moved along that journey. If staff know that something is important to top management they will give it more priority, so it is up to senior managers to keep the spotlight on the service improvement programme and continually re-iterate its importance to the organisation. One very tangible way of doing this is to include customer satisfaction as a key element of staff reward and appraisal strategies. As indicated by Tom Peters in Figure 10.7, customer satisfaction related pay has been relatively common in the USA for some years. In the UK it is still relatively uncommon, so its introduction remains a competitive advantage opportunity for UK organisations seeking leadership positions.

10.5 Conclusions

(a) Key objectives of the quality management system are to demonstrate the organisation's ability to consistently meet customers' requirements and to focus the organisation on the need for continual improvement.

(b) ISO 9004:2000 builds extensively on the continual improvement role of the quality management system and introduces the concepts of interested parties and competitive advantage.

(c) Customer satisfaction is relative. Having satisfied customers may not be enough if your competitors' customers are very satisfied.

(d) Since the Satisfaction Index measures an organisation's success in meeting its customers' requirements, performance can be benchmarked across all industries provided exploratory research has been conducted and the survey was based on what's important to customers.

(e) Comparisons against direct competitors can also be useful for organisations in very competitive markets. For reliable competitor measures a market standing survey must be conducted.

(f) Some organisations are much more successful than others at satisfying customers. The most successful:

1. Have top managers who walk the talk on customer satisfaction.
2. Remind employees constantly about the importance of customers.
3. Use an accurate methodology to measure customer satisfaction.
4. Provide extensive feedback on the results to employees and customers.
5. Make and implement decisions on the PFIs very swiftly after the survey.
6. Keep everyone focused on customer satisfaction between surveys.

(g) According to ISO 9004:2000, the benefits that accrue to organisations that are very successful at satisfying their customers include:

1. Customer loyalty.
2. Repeat business and referral.
3. Operational results such as revenue and market share.
4. Competitive advantage.

Harvard Business School uses the term 'Service-Profit Chain' to describe the positive relationship between customer satisfaction and organisational success. In other words, customer satisfaction pays.

Appendix A

ABC Ltd Customer Survey: Telephone

Classification Data:

Interviewer's name _____ Date: _____ Interviewer No: _____

To be completed by interviewer before the interview

Please tick the appropriate boxes below:

Job function

General Management ☐	Finance ☐	Customer Service ☐	☐
Purchasing	Quality ☐	Sales	
Production	Technical ☐	IT	
Other _____			

Business sector:

Automotive	Electronics ☐	Packaging	☐
Chemicals	Engineering ☐	Plastics	
Computers	Machine Tools ☐	Telecommunications ☐	
Other _____			

Account size:

Large ☐ Medium   ☐ Small   ☐

Introduction

Good morning/afternoon/evening

My name is . . . and I'm ringing from The Leadership Factor on behalf of ABC to find out how satisfied or dissatisfied you are as a customer. I understand you're based at . . . and ABC wrote to you a few days ago asking if you would be prepared to take part in the survey. Is it convenient to run through a few questions with you on the telephone? It will take no more than 10 minutes.

(Agree call back time if necessary)

Section A: Satisfaction

First of all we would like to know how satisfied or dissatisfied you are with

ABC by running through a list of factors and asking you to score each one to indicate your level of satisfaction where 10 would mean totally satisfied and 1 would mean totally dissatisfied.

PROBE SCORES 6 & BELOW

1. On time delivery

2. Product quality

3. Product training provided by ABC

4. Speed of response to enquiries/problems

5. Technical support provided from ABC Service Centres

6. Technical support provided by ABC on your premises

7. Field sales support

8. ABC's ability to innovate

9. Price

10. Lead Times

If any item is scored 6 or lower probe reasons

Item no:	Comments

Section B: Importance

I'd like to consider your requirements as a customer of ABC. If you had to pick out the most important thing to you as a customer what would it be?

Top Priority	

Let's say you had to give . . . **(top priority)** a score between 1 and 10 to indicate how important it is to you, where 10 means 'extremely important' and 1 means 'not at all important', what score would you give it?

Score	

I'm now going to run down the list of requirements again and I'd like you to give a score out of 10 to indicate how important or unimportant each one is to you. When deciding your score, you may find it helpful to compare the importance of the requirement in question with your top priority.

So, compared with . . ., how important or unimportant to you is

1. On time delivery

2. Product quality

3. Product training provided by ABC

4. Speed of response to enquiries/problems

5. Technical support provided from ABC Service Centres

6. Technical support provided by ABC on your premises

7. Field sales support

8. ABC's ability to innovate

9. Price

10. Lead times

Note any additional comments in spaces below:

Item no:	Comments

Section C: ABC Service Centres

Please tick the appropriate box for the ABC Service Centre that you have dealings with

| Birmingham | ☐ | Leeds | ☐ | Newcastle | ☐ |
| Bristol | | Manchester | | Southampton | |

Section D: Priorities for change

I would like you to imagine that you were the Chief Executive of ABC. What changes would you make? It might be helpful to think in terms of urgent, short-term changes and longer-term changes.

Short term

Longer term

Section E: Additional Comments

That's all the questions I have. Do you have any additional comments?

THANK YOU VERY MUCH FOR YOUR HELP.
YOUR VIEWS ARE MUCH APPRECIATED.

Appendix B

ABC Ltd Customer Survey: Self-completion

Introduction and Guidance

The purpose of this survey is to find out what you expect from ABC Ltd as a supplier and how satisfied or dissatisfied you are with the service you receive. We need everyone to answer the questionnaire very honestly, and to encourage this, The Leadership Factor guarantees to protect the identity of everyone who completes it, in accordance with the Market Research Society Code of Conduct.

The questionnaire is divided into two main sections (A and B). Both sections cover the same topics, but in Section A we want to know how **satisfied or dissatisfied** you are with ABC's performance on each factor, and in Section B, how **important or unimportant** each item is to you.

Please complete the questionnaire and return it in the pre paid envelope to The Leadership Factor Ltd by **(date)**

Section A: Satisfaction

We'd like to find out how **satisfied or dissatisfied** you are with the performance of ABC. Please use the scoring guide above and place an X in the relevant box, according to your level of satisfaction, or in the N/A box if you have no experience of that factor. Each factor can be given any score between 1 and 10. It does not matter if some factors have the same score.

1	2	3	4	5	6	7	8	9	10

Totally
dissatisfied
☹

Totally
satisfied
☺

1. On time delivery	N A	1	2	3	4	5	6	7	8	9	10

2. Product quality	N A	1	2	3	4	5	6	7	8	9	10

3. Product training provided by ABC	N A	1	2	3	4	5	6	7	8	9	10
4. Speed of response to enquiries/problems	N A	1	2	3	4	5	6	7	8	9	10
5. Technical support provided from ABC Service Centres	N A	1	2	3	4	5	6	7	8	9	10
6. Technical Support provided by ABC on your premises	N A	1	2	3	4	5	6	7	8	9	10
7. Field sales support	N A	1	2	3	4	5	6	7	8	9	10
8. ABC's ability to innovate	N A	1	2	3	4	5	6	7	8	9	10
9. Price	N A	1	2	3	4	5	6	7	8	9	10
10. Lead times	N A	1	2	3	4	5	6	7	8	9	10

Additional Comments

How to complete Section B

Now we would like to know how **important or unimportant** various requirements are to you as a customer of ABC. Some factors may be more important than others so, first of all, read through all the questions before deciding which is the most important one for you personally. Using the key overleaf as a guide, score the requirement for its importance to you by circling the appropriate number.

Then score all the remaining factors for importance. When deciding your score you may find it helpful to compare each factor with your top priority. Give each factor a score to reflect its importance to you by circling the appropriate number according to the guide below. Each factor can be given any score between 1 and 10. It does not matter if some factors have the same score.

Section B: Importance

How **important or unimportant** are the following factors to you as a customer of ABC:

1	2	3	4	5	6	7	8	9	10

Of no
importance
at all

Extremely
important

1. On time delivery	1	2	3	4	5	6	7	8	9	10
2. Product quality	1	2	3	4	5	6	7	8	9	10
3. Product training provided by ABC	1	2	3	4	5	6	7	8	9	10
4. Speed of response to enquiries/problems	1	2	3	4	5	6	7	8	9	10
5. Technical support provided from ABC Service Centres	1	2	3	4	5	6	7	8	9	10
6. Technical support provided from ABC on your premises	1	2	3	4	5	6	7	8	9	10
7. Field sales support	1	2	3	4	5	6	7	8	9	10
8. ABC's ability to innovate	1	2	3	4	5	6	7	8	9	10
9. Price	1	2	3	4	5	6	7	8	9	10
10. Lead times	1	2	3	4	5	6	7	8	9	10

Additional comments

Section C: ABC Service Centres

Please tick the appropriate box for the ABC Service Centre that you have dealings with

Birmingham ☐   Leeds ☐   Newcastle ☐
Bristol ☐   Manchester ☐   Southampton ☐

Section D: Additional comments

Please use the space below for any additional comments about ABC

Section E: General Information

In this final section, we ask you to give us a few details about yourself. This is important because different groups of customers often have different needs, and it will therefore help us to analyse the survey more accurately.

Which of the following descriptions most accurately fits your job?

General Management	☐	Finance	☐	Customer Service	☐
Purchasing		Quality		Sale	
Production		Technical		IT	

Other _____

Which of the following business sectors is your organisation in?

Automotive	☐	Electronics	☐	Packaging	☐
Chemicals		Engineering		Plastics	
Computers		Machine Tools		Telecommunications	

Other _____

THANK YOU VERY MUCH FOR TAKING THE TIME TO COMPLETE THIS QUESTIONNAIRE YOUR VIEWS ARE MUCH APPRECIATED

Please return your completed questionnaire using the envelope provided (or any other suitable envelope) to the following FREEPOST address: *The Leadership Factor Ltd, FREEPOST Taylor Hill Mill, Huddersfield. HD4 6RS*

Appendix C

ABC Ltd Customer Survey: Internal

Introduction and Guidance

As an employee of 'ABC', we would like to know what your perceptions are of customers' requirements and their satisfaction with ABC. We need everyone to answer the questionnaire very honestly, and to encourage this, The Leadership Factor, our research agency, guarantees to protect the identity of everyone who completes it.

The questionnaire is entirely confidential. When you have completed the questionnaire please seal it in the envelope provided and return it directly to the Leadership Factor.

The questionnaire is divided into two main sections (A and B). Both sections cover the same topics, but in Section A we want to know how **satisfied or dissatisfied** you feel customers are with ABC's performance on each topic and in Section B how **important or unimportant** you believe each factor is to customers.

Please complete the questionnaire and return it by **(date)**

Thank you very much. Your views are much appreciated.

Section A: Satisfaction

First of all we'd like to know how **satisfied** or **dissatisfied** you believe customers are with the performance of ABC. Using the key as a guide, circle the number which best reflects your views. Circle any number between 1 and 10 or circle N/A if you have no experience of the factor concerned

Scoring Guide

1	2	3	4	5	6	7	8	9	10

Totally dissatisfied

Totally satisfied

1. On time delivery	N/A	1	2	3	4	5	6	7	8	9	10
2. Product quality	N/A	1	2	3	4	5	6	7	8	9	10

3. Product training provided by ABC

N A	1	2	3	4	5	6	7	8	9	10

4. Speed of response to enquiries/problems

N A	1	2	3	4	5	6	7	8	9	10

5. Technical support provided from ABC Service Centres

N A	1	2	3	4	5	6	7	8	9	10

6. Technical Support provided by ABC on your premises

N A	1	2	3	4	5	6	7	8	9	10

7. Field sales support

N A	1	2	3	4	5	6	7	8	9	10

8. ABC's ability to innovate

N A	1	2	3	4	5	6	7	8	9	10

9. Price

N A	1	2	3	4	5	6	7	8	9	10

10. Lead times

N A	1	2	3	4	5	6	7	8	9	10

How to complete Section B

Now we would like to know how **important or unimportant** you think various requirements are to customers of ABC. Some requirements may be more important than others. So, first of all, read through all the questions before deciding which you think is the most important one for ABC's customers. Using the key below as a guide, score that requirement for its importance to customers by circling the appropriate number.

   Then score all the remaining requirements for how important or unimportant you think they are to customers. When deciding your score you may find it helpful to compare each requirement with the top priority you identified. Then give each requirement a score to reflect your view of its importance to customers by circling the appropriate number according to the guide below. Each requirement can be given any score between 1 and 10. It does not matter if some of the requirements have the same score.

Scoring Guide

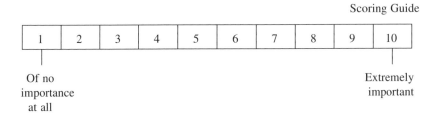

Section B: Importance

How **important or unimportant** are the following factors to you as a customer of ABC:

1	2	3	4	5	6	7	8	9	10

Of no
importance
at all

Extremely
important

1. On time delivery

1	2	3	4	5	6	7	8	9	10

2. Product quality

1	2	3	4	5	6	7	8	9	10

3. Product training
   provided by ABC

1	2	3	4	5	6	7	8	9	10

4. Speed of response to
   enquiries/problems

1	2	3	4	5	6	7	8	9	10

5. Technical support provided
   from ABC Service Centres

1	2	3	4	5	6	7	8	9	10

6. Technical support provided
   from ABC on your premises

1	2	3	4	5	6	7	8	9	10

7. Field sales support

1	2	3	4	5	6	7	8	9	10

8. ABC's ability to innovate

1	2	3	4	5	6	7	8	9	10

9. Price

1	2	3	4	5	6	7	8	9	10

10. Lead times

1	2	3	4	5	6	7	8	9	10

Section C: Additional comments

If you have any additional comments whatsoever regarding the service ABC provide to customers please make use of the space below.

Section D: General Information

In this final section, we ask you to give us a few details about yourself. This is important because it will help us to analyse the survey more accurately.

Which of the following ABC Centres are you based at?

Birmingham	☐	Leeds	☐	Newcastle	☐	
Bristol		Manchester		Southampton		

> **THANK YOU VERY MUCH FOR TAKING THE TIME TO COMPLETE THIS QUESTIONNAIRE**
> **YOUR VIEWS ARE MUCH APPRECIATED**

Please return your completed questionnaire using the envelope provided
(or any other suitable envelope) to the following
FREEPOST address:
The Leadership Factor
FREEPOST
Taylor Hill Mill
Huddersfield
HD4 6RS

Index